To my mother, who taught me to read and write, and to my father, who taught me to watch and listen

Chapter 1: The Day the Music Lived

Only moments earlier, she had been crying, shaking and screaming at the mere thought of seeing her idol – just like a Beatle-crazed fan straight out of "A Hard Day's Night."

But now 8-year-old Ella provided a picture of poise for the dozens of snapping, whirring and flashing cameras, chatting easily and joking with the man whose right arm wrapped her waist: Paul McCartney.

"Hello, Dad," Paul said moments later, pumping my hand. But it wasn't my day – it was Ella's.

And I was never prouder to be "Dad."

The dates that stick in the memory tend to be the good (birthdays and wedding anniversaries), the bad (deaths and catastrophes), and the not-always-so-good anymore (birthdays and wedding anniversaries).

Let's be blunt: the bad dates stand out on par with the celebratory ones, especially in the collective memory. For every July 4, 1776, June 6, 1944, and July 20, 1969, there's a Dec. 7, 1941, Nov. 22, 1963, and Sept. 11, 2001 (notice how even the "good" dates are war-related – the moon landing, after all, was as much about the arms race as new frontiers).

For fans of the Beatles, whose every move as a group has been chronicled day-by-day (July 15, 1963: Paul was fined 15 quid for speeding!), there's one date that overshadows the others, more so than the day John met Paul (July 6, 1957), the band's first "Ed Sullivan Show" appearance (Feb. 9, 1964) or their birthdays (Ringo: July 7, 1940; John: Oct. 9, 1940; Paul: June 18, 1942; George: Feb. 25, 1943, though recent evidence suggests he was really born late on Feb. 24).

Ask any Beatles fan – especially those of us who can prattle on about the great George birthday debate – the most significant date in the group's history. The honest answer will be Dec. 8, 1980. If you have to ask what happened that day (or night, actually), you shouldn't be reading this book. Or, then again, maybe you really need to.

For my adolescence and adulthood into fatherhood, the events of Dec. 8, 1980, defined my life as a Beatles fan – too young to have any memories of them together as a band, but old enough to feel the aching loss of something I would never experience. But not for lack of trying: I read every book. I learned to play every song. I retraced the Beatles' footsteps in London and Liverpool, first on my honeymoon with a woman who shares my obsession, and later with our daughter, Ella, who has been raised a Beatle baby since her birth in 1997. In some ways, we're a family of seven.

For Ella, Dec. 8, 1980, is an abstraction – sad, but ancient history, really. The Beatles date that matters most to her is Oct. 3, 2005: the day she met Paul McCartney and took her mother, Theresa, and me along on her golden ticket to ride.

In our humble Brooklyn home, it's a date that's greeted like a birthday or an anniversary – the kind that will never get old or dreaded. Oct. 3, 2005, represents an affirmation of what we love about the Beatles and marks a highlight in our ongoing journey as a family bonded by music as much as by blood.

It took me 25 years, save a couple of months, to realize the Beatles aren't about an unobtainable past as much as about finding unexpected joy in the moment – and, as scary as the thought can be at times, embracing the future (because, after all, tomorrow never knows).

Even in the era of iPods, the Beatles are an experience best shared – whether it's at a fan convention crammed with a multi-generational mélange of Beatlemaniacs or a slightly eccentric Brooklyn family of three singing "Help!" at the top of their lungs at the start of another road trip, drowning out the rumble of passing tractor trailers on the New Jersey Turnpike.

Our ongoing journey has taken us to Rockefeller Plaza, where Theresa and I rolled 4-year-old Ella in her stroller before dawn on a sweltering August morning to see Ringo perform a mini-concert on the "Today" show; to Beatle landmarks in Hamburg, London and Liverpool, where Ella became pals with the sweet elderly woman who lives in Ringo's boyhood home; to encounters with Yoko Ono, who gave Ella perhaps the best answer yet to the question, "Why did the Beatles break up?" And, of course, to Ella's quixotic meeting with Paul, a story she'll dine out on for the rest of her life.

On a blistering summer day, nearly four years after Ella met Paul, we got word through Beatle-fan circles that he planned to perform a surprise set atop the ancient marquee of the Ed Sullivan Theater on Broadway as part of an appearance on "Late Show with David Letterman." Subsequent Internet chatter, though, suggested the gig had been canceled because of safety concerns. But Theresa insisted we press on.

I left work early. Theresa and I picked up Ella from her School of Rock summer day camp, just blocks from the theater. We arrived to find the street packed with about 4,000 fans. Some 46 years to the day Paul got fined 15 quid for speeding, he stopped traffic on Broadway.

The three of us, New Yorkers undaunted by crowds, secured a perch virtually under the marquee. "You know, we're not going to be able to see anything here," Ella, by then 12 and believing she was 30, scoffed as she glared through her horn-rimmed librarian glasses, held up by her button nose and chubby cheeks.

"Yeah, but this is as close to him as we'll ever get," I said without thinking, a recurring theme in my family life.

"Oh, like we haven't been closer to him than this," she shot back, her icy mockery tumbling onto the hot July sidewalk and melting in an embarrassing puddle at my feet.

"I meant this is the closest we'll ever be to him singing," I parried, but knew the match was lost.

The moment summed up much for me: how lucky we've been. How Theresa's insistence on pushing ahead continues to be the force that makes our luck, trumping my journalist's reflexive skepticism. How our daughter is changing with age, starting with sarcasm, surely to soon morph into mutiny and about a decade of all-out war. Only she'll have to find something other than rock and roll to fuel her inevitable rebellion against us.

Ella stood amid the eager crowd, a too-cool-for-school, seen-it-all look plastered across her red, slightly sunburned face. "Do we really have to wait here?" she asked, gripping the black-and-white "Abbey Road" silhouette tote bag slung over her right shoulder.

Seconds later, Paul crawled out a second-story window and onto the overhang. We only could see the occasional wave of his hand, or the top of his Hofner violin bass peek out over the marquee. But we heard his voice: "I've played some strange places in my time," he quipped.

He ripped into "Get Back," and Broadway became the Cavern Club. Ella couldn't contain her smile or stop from dancing and singing. The CBS pages lined up in front of us, none much older than 20, knew all the words. Even some of the cops were singing and trying hard not to wriggle along.

Another special day. Another memory we'll always have, no matter what comes our way. Something worth sharing.

After the seven-song mini-concert, Ella grabbed my Blackberry and posted to her Facebook page, telling her friends to look for us in the crowd during that night's broadcast. As the tallest member of our trio, I was the beacon: "Look for my dad. For those of you who don't know him, my dad is bald."

Seeing and hearing the discovery of the Beatles through fresh eyes and ears is life affirming, and offers a sense of renewal, especially for those of us for whom hair is but a memory. Dig a little deeper, and the band's journey – the struggles, triumphs, friendships, marriages, breakups and tragedies – is life's path writ large, filled with lessons we'll probably ignore and pitfalls we'll stumble into anyway, because that's human nature. But knowing their story makes John, Paul, George and Ringo all the more human to us.

More than four decades after their final walk across Abbey Road, the Beatles still matter. If music, as the scientists tell us, is good for the brain, then the Beatles also are good for the soul – and for bringing people together. A 2009 Pew Research Center survey suggests what fans already know: the Beatles, blamed by some for creating the generation gap in the 1960s, have helped bridge the chasm, at least musically. The group ranked in the top four favorite acts of Americans 16 to 64.

Part of the responsibility of being a fan is helping keep the group's music and story alive as new generations embark on their own Beatlesque journeys with the calendar not mattering as much as what lies ahead. Every family is a magical mystery tour. *Raising a Beatle Baby* is ours. So roll up, step on the gas and wipe that tear away...

Chapter 2: Two of Us

You don't set out to raise a Beatle baby – it's not like religion where you have serious, heartfelt discussions beforehand about the child's spiritual fate (*Well, you're Jewish and I'm Episcopalian, so why don't we split the difference and raise little Milhouse a Hindu!*). The Beatles are just a fact of life in our house: in the music blaring from our stereo, the posters on our walls, the books on our shelves, the songs we sing and play on the various instruments that pack our living room (kazoo solo, anyone?).

I can't tell you my first Beatles memory – they always were just kind of there for me. But not so much in my childhood home in Brooklyn, where the family "hi-fi" gained most of its employment playing comedy records – Bob Newhart, Bill Cosby, highlights from "All in the Family," my father's (and the country's) favorite TV show.

My parents, Marie, a public school teacher and voracious reader, and Andy, a postal worker and television and movie obsessive, didn't play a lot of music. Our radio generally blared news talk shows. When my folks did bring out the tunes, they didn't rock much harder than Bing Crosby – typical of Depression children like them, but far mellower than many of my friends' parents, who were borderline Baby Boomers. The closest thing in my parents' record collection to rock and roll was an album by the Lemon Pipers, the one-hit wonders behind the 1967 folk-pseudo-psychedelic-bubblegum treacle "Green Tambourine." I don't remember Ma and Da ever actually playing it.

I was born in Brooklyn, in the summer of 1966, about two weeks before the U.S. release of "Revolver." My brother, Drew, arrived exactly 54 weeks later, smack in the Summer of Love with "Sgt. Pepper's Lonely Hearts Club Band" No. 1 on the charts. If our parents weren't rocking, they were definitely rolling.

There was little room for the Beatles in our modest Sunset Park apartment, which my sister, Rosie, brought to the bursting point with her arrival in 1971. But plenty of Fab Four exposure seeped in from the outside.

There were the records Aunt Rose, my mother's kid sister, played on her real stereo, built from a kit by her brother, my Uncle Tommy. Aunt Rose, barely 13 when the Beatles debuted on "The Ed Sullivan Show," rode the Beatlemania wave into adulthood. I'd soak in the album covers, devouring the liner notes and annotated track lists (Paul played "fuzz bass" on "Think for Yourself," according to the back of "Rubber Soul." I still don't know what fuzz bass is). Most kids gravitate toward "Yellow Submarine," but the hazier seas of "I Want You (She's so Heavy)" enveloped me.

Between both sides of the family, I had 20 cousins, most older than I and well steeped in Beatledom. A cube-like mobile constructed with the four headshots that came with the White Album dangled from my Aunt Mickey's living room ceiling. Her son, Raffael, (in Brooklyn, we called him Ralphie) could play all the songs on piano and guitar, turning family visits into

Beatle sing-alongs and helping inspire my determination to make music.

There was the jukebox in Jimmy's Pizzeria, a block from our apartment, one of the two places we would occasionally go to dinner (the other was a nearby Chinese restaurant – the only one in a neighborhood that years later would become New York's third Chinatown). Jimmy's jukebox sucked many of my quarters playing Paul's 1971 hit "Uncle Albert/Admiral Halsey," and reissues of "Got to Get You Into My Life" and "Helter Skelter." (Though, in full disclosure, I probably spent more of my parents' change on Ray Stevens' 1974 novelty hit "The Streak" than all the Beatles songs combined.)

I couldn't escape the Beatles, even at my grammar school, St. Agatha's, where they taught a fourth R – repression. Our music teacher, Sister Mary Beata ("That's B-e-a-t-a. And if you step out of line, I'm gonna beat-a you."), was a phenomenal musician and singer, who released albums that earned her the moniker "The Singing Nun" (okay, she wasn't the first to get the title, but it fit).

She terrified me. The thought of her still does. Like Monty Python's Dinsdale Piranha, she wielded sarcasm and the threat of violence as weapons. If you starred in her twice-annual musical pageants (Christmas and St. Patrick's Day), sang at the children's 9 a.m. Sunday Mass, or played in her folk Mass group, she ran you hard. But you at least were assured a spot on what passed for her good side. If not, watch out.

The thought of singing in front of others petrified me. I couldn't play any instruments. Mass bored me, and I rarely made it before the final 12:30 p.m. service, even though I spent half my childhood on the same block as our church.

Sister Beata sometimes seemed to go out of her way to humiliate certain people, and I absorbed the brunt a couple of times. I surely will be hunted and beaten for even suggesting she's anything less than a saint: Sister Mary Beata is beloved by legions of parents and former students whose lives were enriched by a school that gave working-class kids a quality education. I recognize the value in carefully meted out tough love. But it never worked on me.

It's fair to say, though, that Sister Beata changed my life: When I was in third grade, she played Side A of "Revolver" for our class.

Sure, I'd heard "Yellow Submarine" many times. But the rest blew my 8-year-old mind. The crisp, searing chords of "Taxman." The pulsing strings of "Eleanor Rigby" weaving through my ears and seeping into uncharted folds of my brain. "Here, There and Everywhere," the sweetest, lushest sound I had ever heard, threatening to ferry me out of the classroom on a cotton-candy cloud.

All my experiences with the Beatles, up to that point, were outside the home. But soon I would have my own music.

Aunt Rose lived with my kindly grandfather on the top floor of the two-family Brooklyn house where my mother grew up with an extended family of never-married eccentrics. My mother's Aunt Flo, a short, rotund woman filled a 6-by-8 room set up so she didn't have to move from her bed to do anything except go to church Bingo games. Her occasional winnings paid for the full line of Nabisco cookies and hand-dipped chocolates she kept at her bedside, and generously shared with visitors. Aunt Flo's previous career involved selling squishy rubber doorknob covers.

Her brother, Uncle Rocco, a radio repairman turned TV repairman, rarely bothered to open the shop he ran on McDonald Avenue, where customers would leave their broken sets in front of the locked door. He'd eventually get around to fixing the radios and televisions between trips to the track.

In retirement – at least his official retirement – he pretty much kept to his room, piled with tubes and old radios, along with an easel and paints (he actually was quite talented: he once painted a replica of DaVinci's "The Last Supper," which was near perfect, except that St. Peter looked a lot like a skinny old, bald Italian guy from Brooklyn named Rocco).

Rocco, the forgotten apostle, delved into his junk pile one day and pulled out for me my first radio. It was an early transistor model from the 1960s, roughly the shape of a Kindle, but as thick as "War and Peace" and puke green. It only got AM, but I didn't care. He gave me an earplug that I used to listen when I should have been sleeping, letting me absorb the Top 40 hits on WABC and WNBC, and catch Met games on WHN, which played country music when the Amazins' weren't losing.

In the fall of 1975, during the first season of

"Saturday Night Live," in which Lorne Michaels offered the Beatles $3,000 to reunite ("If you want to give less to Ringo, that's up to you"), my parents scraped up a little more than that for a down payment on a home. We moved from our cramped apartment to a three-bedroom row house two blocks away. Not long after, a gang of kids, probably all of 13 years old, robbed me of the radio at knifepoint (a switchblade) on our stoop.

But I soon inherited the family hi-fi and started buying records – Queens' "Bohemian Rhapsody," my first 45, got a dizzying turntable workout. I saved for my own stereo, put over my goal by confirmation gifts (going to church was good for something, after all), and embarked on building my Beatles record collection.

To save the 50-cent bus fare, my friends and I would walk a couple miles to 86th Street, the main shopping strip in Bay Ridge. We'd hang out at Record Factory, and our favorite, the aptly named Little Record Store, a sliver of a shop where musician types would strike cool poses to best show off denim jackets with Led Zeppelin album covers rendered in runny acrylic paint on the back.

It was less a record store than a refuge. We were at the dawn of the "Saturday Night Fever" era, where rock vs. disco became the cultural and social dividing line, pitting flannel-shirt-clad hicks (rockers) vs. leather-jacket-wearing cuigines (a bastardization of *cugino*, Italian for "cousin," and Brooklyn shorthand for Tony Manero wannabes). My Beatles-loving friends and I stood in the middle of the battlefield – much of "Saturday Night Fever" was filmed in Bay Ridge, and we bowled across the street from the disco where John Travolta and the Bee Gees made their indelible pop-cultural imprint.

At the same time, hip-hop began to spring around us. The new beat of the Sugarhill Gang's "Rapper's Delight" filled our neighborhood as boom boxes that dwarfed my beloved, forever-lost radio proliferated. Some of my pals travelled lugging increasing thick portable stereos and flattened cardboard boxes, which provided convenient padding for impromptu break-dancing showdowns in the local junior high schoolyard, feet from the ever-present potheads blasting Black Sabbath. We only read about Sid killing Nancy and CBGB pulsing to punk in Manhattan, which might as well have been across the Atlantic Ocean, instead of the East River.

The Beatles didn't quite fit into this world. Sure, Paul produced silly loves songs, but the group generally wasn't big news anymore. The New York Post's September 1979 tease of a headline – "The Beatles Are Back," about plans for a supposed United Nations save-the-world concert in New York – turned out to be bogus (and gave me an early lesson about being damn careful about what you put in the newspaper).

Being Beatles fans made us more misfits than rebels. I wanted Beatle-like long hair, which by the late 1970s wasn't revolution as much as the style among the middle-aged. A mop-top, though, wouldn't fly at St. Agatha's where anything so much as a strand touching the ears was anathema for boys.

Eighth-grade graduation came as a relief. My

parents, at my request, bought me a small acoustic guitar, with a fake rosewood veneer, very Roy Rogers-looking, for $30 out of the Sears catalogue. My musical exploits at that point had been limited to picking out simple tunes on the old Lowery organ given to us by my mother's Aunt Anna, the old maid sister of Flo and Rocco, and perhaps the oddest, if most functional, of the trio. She had enjoyed a successful career in the garment trade. But she dressed like a pauper in faded floral housedresses, drank red wine with ice, and filled her bedroom with statues of saints – boasting she'd arranged them so she'd never sleep with her feet to them (especially not her favorite, St. Anthony, the patron saint of lost items).

Within days, my guitar became a near-lost item when I tossed it into our basement. Nobody told me that my fingers would bleed, let alone ache. Try as I might, I couldn't tune the thing and kept popping strings, occasionally getting lashed across the face. The only sound the guitar made came from me whacking it in frustration.

By the end of the summer, though, I could pluck out the odd melody and play a couple simple chords, thanks to a beginner's instruction book my mother bought for me. I even began to look the part of a would-be rocker – I lost much of my baby fat as my hair grew over my ears and crept toward my shoulders. My new school, Bishop Ford, employed a moderate dress code (no sneakers, jeans or T-shirts), with no stifling uniforms or restrictions on hair length. The faculty was a relatively mellow mix of lay teachers (called such, we used to say, because they were allowed to get laid) and well-traveled missionary monks, priests and nuns, most of whom didn't wear habits.

I appreciated the discipline and order with no real threat of violence or humiliation. I quickly became comfortable enough to stay once a week to take a guitar class. After learning new chords, I'd run home to figure out some simple Beatles songs – "Love Me Do" to start. By that November, I became determined to get an electric guitar, and convinced my mother to buy me one for Christmas – and even order it early to beat the holiday rush.

We returned to the Sears catalogue and picked out a knockoff version of a Gibson Les Paul starburst guitar for about $100, which also would more than cover my birthday present the following July. The guitar arrived the first week of December 1980 with a hard-shell case and a six-watt amp outfitted with a distortion button that made my thrashing sound awe-inspiring – at least to me. My father would stomp on the living room floor above my basement room to get me to stop, more annoyed at my attempts to sing than my strumming ("Hey, Bob Dyin' – shut up!").

A couple days after getting my prized guitar, I had off from school for the Feast of the Immaculate Conception, which falls on Dec. 8. I spent the day on 86th Street with my pals, and bought the "Help!" album. Between us, my brother and I now owned every Beatles LP. It was time to start buying the solo albums. John had just released his first record in five years. The single, "(Just Like) Starting Over," sounded pretty good.

Maybe I'd pick up the "Double Fantasy" album next...

The Beatles were beginning a long residency at Hamburg's recently opened Star-Club in April 1962, when nearly 4,000 miles away in Cape May Courthouse, N.J., Theresa was born three months premature.

The Beatles always were there for her, too – and not all that much in her house in suburban New Jersey, just outside Philadelphia. Her first Beatles memory stands out, in retrospect, as an unlikely one: a family car ride sing-along of "Can't Buy Me Love" led by her mother, Henrietta – known to all as Hank, who grew up worshipping at the altar of Sinatra in South Philly. Then again, Hank, a boisterous, garrulous and blunt-spoken woman who exhales unvarnished opinion and puffs of cigarette smoke in the same breath, always liked belting a good song, dating from her days as a saloon singer in the 1940s.

Almost certainly not singing was Theresa's father, John, a taciturn tugboat captain with a withering glare that allowed him to be heard without speaking. His relentless stare frightened away some boyfriends, including some of the boys in Beatle bands Theresa would sneak out of the house to chase as a teen. Many grown men were frightened of John, but children were able to see through a tough exterior that belied an unusually reserved man who would leave the room rather than let anyone see him laugh or tear up at a birthday card from his children.

John's sensitive side shone through most in his relationship with his youngest child and closest companion, Frankie, who arrived about two months after I did in 1966. Frankie, born with Down syndrome, nearly didn't make it through his first day. The doctors said he wouldn't last six months and tried to have him institutionalized. Hank and John, though barely scarping by at times, refused – a stubbornness and resolve they passed onto Frankie, Theresa and older brother Jay.

Frankie's biggest challenges were physical – a hole in his heart and weak lungs made it tough at times to run, let alone walk. But he made it to a school for special children his father helped build, and went on to compete in the Special Olympics, even amid frequent hospitalizations and painful blood treatments. He shared his mother's tart tongue and his father's glare, combined with a sense of humor all his own. "How sweet it is!" he'd crack in his best Jackie Gleason, when stuck in the hospital that was his second home.

Like his sister and brother, who played guitar, Frankie found joy in music. He'd sit for hours cross-legged, nestled behind the living room couch, in front of his stereo, headphones on and child-sized guitar in hand, strumming and singing as he listened to cassettes of Elvis and Roy Orbison – "Only the Lonely" was a favorite. It was as if he were transported to a recording studio in his mind – even if unfamiliar passers-by might not hear recognizable music in the frequent "performances" that wafted out the bay window onto the sleepy suburban street outside.

Theresa, amid her brother's illness and some rough economic times for her family, found refuge in music and the arts. She threw herself into dance be-

ginning as a pre-schooler, studying ballet. Part of her
hand-me-downs from older cousins included Beatles
singles, dating to the pre-British Invasion Decca and
Vee-Jay label releases.

All the illness and uncertainty around her im-
bued Theresa with a fascination with death, a self-suf-
ficient feistiness and the same mordant sense of humor
that kept her parents going. Hank and John would joke
about who would die first as they drained endless pots
of Maxwell House coffee and inhaled cartons of Marl-
boros while tending to Frankie, sometimes around the
clock. Theresa's taste for the macabre brought her at
age 12 to read Los Angeles prosecutor Vincent Bugli-
osi's book "Helter Skelter," about the Manson Family
murders, raising her interest in the Beatles to a new, if
decidedly morbid level. She saved to buy the White Album, along with the so-called "Red" and "Blue" albums,
in her own private patriotic joke reflecting the fervor
enveloping nearby Philadelphia with the nation's bi-
centennial approaching in 1976.

She stuck with dancing and moved into singing
and acting during high school, taking her performing
from school plays to dinner theater gigs. She joined
her dance troupe on the stage of Radio City Music Hall
with Lionel Hampton, and would reprise the performance at Ronald Reagan's inauguration in 1980, to the
dual delight and mortification of her staunchly Demo-
cratic parents.

Theresa graduated high school voted Most
Likely to Succeed, but either didn't get into or couldn't
afford the colleges where she wanted to pursue per-

forming arts. She decided to take a year off from school, get a job, save some money and figure out what to do with her life. She worked a pre-dawn shift making sandwiches for vending machines, standing hairnet-to-hairnet with a mix of life-hardened older women she found wise and amusing.

On the night of Dec. 8, 1980, she went to bed early. As her father drove her to work at about 4 a.m. the next morning, she heard the news on the radio. She walked into the shop in a daze, greeted by animated chatter.

"Who cares about some dead hippie?" one of the old ladies scoffed to general agreement.

Theresa quit as soon after and enrolled in college, determined to study the arts and move to New York.

Chapter 3: Come Together

She inspired a mix of desire and fascination at first sight – a dark-eyed, curvy beauty, part Elizabeth Taylor, part Judy Garland, with an aura of cool that swept up through her punk-short, spiky dark-brown hair. I found excuses to frequently walk by the new girl's cubicle at the Manhattan accounting firm where I was working my way through college in the mid-1980s, ferrying copies of tax returns around the office.

Theresa rarely looked up from proofreading financial statements awash with endless lines of transactions, each involving sums that dwarfed our yearly earnings. Not that I had much to complain about – sure, I was 19 and living in my parents' basement. But I also was fortunate enough to be studying Politics and Journalism at NYU on a generous scholarship – and to have a job that helped pay the balance of the tuition bill.

Some months earlier, while making deliveries as a minimum-wage ($3.35 an hour) foot messenger, I managed to talk my way into a $6-an-hour, 30-hour-a-week office boy job at one of our customers, an accounting firm whose best-known client was Merv Griffin (whom, I'd learn later, once interviewed the Beatles). The office was just two blocks away from the Daily News Building – where "Superman" was filmed, where I had delivered press releases and where I dreamed of working one day for my hometown paper.

Theresa, 23 and armed with a theater degree from Rutgers, carved out a new life as an office drone by day, playwright by night. She wasn't far removed from the knee surgery that put a definitive close to her dancing career, though it unofficially ended a couple years earlier when she auditioned for a Broadway show that had made a singular sensation. The casting director turned to a colleague and sniped, "They grow them big in Jersey, don't they?"

She never turned around when I'd walk by, no matter how much noise I'd make. She tuned out the world with her new-fangled Walkman. I figured, given the haircut, she was listening to some edgy New Wave tunes. I could have sworn, though, I once heard the psychedelic guitar lick that opens "She Said, She Said," from "Revolver," escape from the headphones she used to tune out the world.

To her, I was, at best, a mildly amusing, scruffy college kid with a picture of a girlfriend on his desk. We'd chat and joke sometimes, and occasionally eat lunch with mutual work friends, but that was it.

I left the firm in 1987, after saving enough not only to work for free as a summer intern at a chain of small Manhattan papers, but to pay NYU $1,200 for the privilege. Money be damned – the opportunity thrilled me. I'd learned that life tethered to a desk – especially helping other people count their cash– wasn't for me.

By the following summer, I was out of school, making $250 a week as the sole fulltime reporter for the Battery News, a start-up paper covering the then–

nascent neighborhood of Battery Park City, in the shadow of the World Trade Center. I bounced between crowded sublets and my parents' house, happy to be working hard at something I loved. Theresa also had moved on – to another accounting firm, making more money as a secretary and later as an office manager. After some back and forth between her parents' home two hours away, she settled into a nice, if small, apartment in Brooklyn Heights, a relatively safe part of then-dangerous New York.

I bounded into Penn Station early on the Saturday morning of Labor Day weekend 1988, a few weeks after my 22nd birthday. I manically walked up and down the platform, if only to stay awake. After closing the latest edition of the Battery News the night before, I bar-hopped until the wee hours, stumbled back to the Greenwich Village sublet studio apartment I shared with a pal and collapsed onto my used Styrofoam futon.

I already was regretting agreeing to go to the Jersey Shore to play in a charity volleyball tournament organized by Shari, the girlfriend of my best buddy from the accounting firm, Marc. I hated the beach, and while I was far better at sports than I looked, we never played much volleyball on the streets of Brooklyn.

I also possessed a Woody Allen-like phobia about leaving the city, and didn't know how to dress, even for something as informal as beach volleyball – though I suspected the coral T-shirt that suddenly was starting to look very pink, powder-blue shorts and black hi-top Converse sneakers might not have been the most appropriate ensemble. I wasn't sure if I was in the right place – I knew every graffiti-smeared inch of the subways, but had never taken a commuter rail train alone before. They didn't mark these platforms properly, trains were always switching tracks, you could never hear the announcements clearly, do I even have the right ticket?...

"Hey, Jere!"

Standing in front of me was a smiling Theresa, her dark hair still short, if no longer dangerously spiky. She wore dark-grey pants with the bottoms rolled up mid-calf, and a dark-blue hooded sweatshirt emblazoned with her first name in script white stitching, a remnant from her days waitressing on a drafty old, four-mast ship docked on the Philadelphia waterfront. Marc mentioned she might come, but I hadn't given it much thought. The silver NJTransit train pulled in and we got on. We sat next to one another in back of a rear car. She curled her legs under her, and we eased into conversation.

Her friendly, relaxed demeanor surprised me. I found it more inviting than the from-afar edginess that excited me in whole different way. I knew she was into theater. I was barely out of NYU, so I had no problem faking my way through pretentious textbook-y conversations on the arts. Plus, I'd seen a bunch of shows through discount tickets offered by the student union. We'd both recently attended that summer's Shakespeare in the Park edition of "Much Ado About Nothing," with Kevin Kline.

"Shakespeare's all well and fine," I said. "But I like Kline a lot better in 'A Fish Called Wanda.' And John Cleese is funnier than Shakespeare will ever be."

Theresa giggled and proceeded to give me a gentle lesson on all things theater. She seemed mildly entertained as I babbled about my job, describing how my story about the closure of beloved local movie theater became international news, how I'd uncovered a brothel operating in a residential building in the then-burgeoning neighborhood of Tribeca. She divided her free time between writing plays in a genre I'd later dub blue collar surreal and volunteering at Gay Men's Health Crisis, serving as a "buddy" to people with AIDS.

Despite my disdain for the beach, I played the volleyball of my life, hurling myself like a ragdoll into the icky, dreaded sand – even if Theresa, sitting on the sidelines, barely looked up from writing in her spiral notebook, with its doodle-speckled yellow cover. As I brushed away the sand, I wondered why I found myself showing off for someone who didn't seem to care about anything other than the show unfolding in her notebook.

That night, after getting cleaned up, we piled into the Olde Queens Tavern, an ancient New Brunswick pub that looked – and smelled, thanks to a permanent odor of stale beer – its age. The joint, just starting to fill with returning Rutgers University students, was a favorite of Marc and Shari, who had whittled away much of their college glory days there not all that long before. Over pitchers of Budweiser we played a drinking game that involved going around guessing every-body's answer to a question. Favorite Beatle came up quickly enough. I guessed John for Theresa. Wrong.

"I'm a George girl," she said. Chugged a beer.

She guessed John for me. "It's a lot more com-plicated than that, but if absolutely forced to narrow the four inextricable parts of the whole down to one, yes, it would be John," I babbled. Another beer.

That led to favorite Beatles album. I pegged Theresa for a "Sgt. Pepper" fan. "Wrong again," she said, grinning. "Try 'Revolver.'"

I tried to delay another chugfest, amid growing wooziness. I wasn't sure if I was intoxicated as much by the beer as by the beautiful Beatles-loving woman on the other side of the worn, scratch-filled wooden table.

"At best, 'Revolver' is transition album between 'Rubber Soul' and 'Pepper,'" I argued. "How can you like an album with practically no John songs?"

She laughed. I still had to drink that Bud.

Marc and Shari drove us back to Brooklyn, and I got a friendly hug from Theresa before she dashed out of the car, across Henry Street and into her building. I couldn't stop thinking about her after that weekend, but figured that was it – at best, maybe we'd run into each other sometime. After all, I was a boy (though I'd managed not to mention my age – with my hairline in the early stages of recession, I easily passed for my late 20s) about to move back into my parents' basement. She was a woman with a real job and an apartment.

The next week, I was set to go a Mets game with

Marc, but he had to back out with little notice. I called various friends, with no luck. Marc suggested I ask Theresa, which excited and terrified me. She'd never want to go with me. We got into this whole high school I-think-she-likes-you thing. I summoned the courage to call her just hours before the game and she said yes.

We sat together in the late summer chill, as the breeze took wings off Flushing Bay and lashed those of us in the cheap seats. She wore a black sweater she'd bought at the Gap in Greenwich Village before meeting me on a subway platform. I chattered in my T-shirt and shorts. She pretended to be interested in the game and I got to sound like an authority on something I actually knew a lot about. On the way back from the game, I was supposed to get off the R train at Eighth Street, but made some last-minute excuse about needing to go one more stop to get to a store that was open late. I got off at Prince Street and jumped back on just as the doors were closing.

"It's after 11 o'clock, I think it'd be safer if I saw you home," I told her.

As we got to her door, she invited me in. "You want some ice cream?" she asked. "You like Ben & Jerry's Chubby Hubby?"

When she went into the kitchen, I checked out the album collection that filled much of the row of white Ikea shelves that lined one wall of her living room. She owned even more LPs than I did, and with a far greater variety – Broadway cast albums and jazz records, heavy on the Ella Fitzgerald, all in alphabetical order, by artist. With one exception: The Beatles albums were first, in order of release, followed by solo albums, starting with John and moving to Paul to George to Ringo – just like the way I filed mine. She saw me looking, pulled out "Revolver," and put it on the turntable. She had two copies – she played a recently re-released version of the original British pressing, with three additional songs, all great Lennon compositions: "Dr. Robert," "And Your Bird Can Sing" and "I'm Only Sleeping." I suddenly understood what she'd meant.

I couldn't sleep that night – and not because of my excitement about the Mets going up 11 games on the second-place Pirates. I'd thought I'd been in love before, but never felt anything like this. I was too scared, though, to even contemplate a next move.

Theresa took the initiative and called me a couple days later, causing my heart to all but leap out of my chest at the sound her voice. "It's my turn to take you out," she said. "Your choice."

I took a chance and went for the quirky – a double feature at the Film Forum, an art film house in a former garage near the entrance to the perennially packed Holland Tunnel. Instead of the usual artsy-fartsy fare, the Film Forum was showing a 1950s Vincent Price double feature: "13 Ghosts" and "The Tingler." Both were products of the delightfully twisted mind of campy horror director William Castle, known for filling both his movies and the theaters they played in with cheesy special effects.

Theresa's laughter echoed through the movie house as secretly wired seats vibrated like joy buzzers when "The Tingler" got loose in the theater, and when the baker's dozen of ghosts – sheets on clotheslines rigged from the top of the screen – streaked over our heads. I was glad she liked the movies, and even happier to be with someone who shared my offbeat sense of humor. We walked the streets for hours after, talking about life, family and dreams, becoming friends.

In the coming days, we took turns finding excuses to hang out – a quick bite here, a movie there. I brought my acoustic guitar to her house one night. I wasn't great, but could play all the Beatles songs without looking at the music, which I couldn't read anyway. She could sing all the songs without looking at the words. If her laughter filled my soul, her beautiful soprano voice rendered my knees weak and my heart strong. I wanted to hold her hand. I grabbed for hers just she reached for mine.

Awoken by a clatter of footsteps, I looked up to see a blur in a red Minnie Mouse T-shirt bound into the next room. I shook my head, unsure of where I was as an unusually bright fall sun beamed through the window hard up against the unfamiliar bed. As I groggily reached for my glasses, I heard a needle hit a record in the adjoining room, followed a few scratchy seconds later by "I've Just Seen a Face" – the opening cut of the American version of "Rubber Soul."

I knew I was home.

The soundtrack for our romance, though, proved to be a new album – "The Traveling Wilburys, Vol. 1," by the greatest supergroup of them all: George,

Bob Dylan, Tom Petty, Jeff Lynne and Roy Orbison, who, Theresa told me, was one of Frankie's favorites. Roy, in his ethereal voice, both sad and powerful, sang of love and loneliness in "Handle With Care," a George tune that quickly became our favorite cut from the album.

Theresa survived an initial encounter with my family, and was prepping me for meeting hers at Christmas. We were excited about the trip, as well as our plans to go together to Strawberry Fields for the annual Dec. 8 vigil. On the morning before, Theresa's white Panasonic clock radio went off as always at 6 a.m., set to WNEW-FM, then the city's premier classic rock station. Usually animated morning show sidekick Marty Martinez solemnly delivered the sad news of Orbison's sudden death of a heart attack at age 52. We clutched one another, and lie silently, in an odd bonding moment.

Unknown to Theresa, I'd already bought her present – a CD player that cost me a week's salary. I also purchased some discs, starting with "Revolver." I made sure to quickly get a couple of Orbison albums.

I gave it all to her on Christmas morning in her parents' home (we slept in bunk beds, with Theresa and Frankie sharing the top bunk). I passed a baptism of fire that included her father's glare, which I effectively countered with a goofy grin. Her mother loved newspapers and politics, so I listened as she talked. Frankie and I bonded over the TV shows we both grew up watching – though we argued bitterly over his assertion that Don Knotts was a funnier foil than Norman Fell on "Three's Company." Slamming his hand on the coffee table for emphasis, he declared, "Furley is better than Roper – end of story!"

As Frankie went from pale to red and back again, Theresa stopped me from pressing on: "You're going to give him another heart attack!"

I left determined to start saving for my next big purchase: an engagement ring.

We married just shy of the second anniversary of our reconnection at the beach. We didn't have much of a budget, but decided to go for campy glitz, picking Philadelphia's Mummers Museum, a celebration of the city's annual New Years Day parade that features comical marching bands in elaborate feather-bedecked costumes strutting down Broad Street to "Golden Slippers." We were determined to have live music, though we pretty early on ruled out an all-Beatles band – the wedding, after all, was about more than just us. But we knew what wanted for our first dance.

"You sure about that?" Tony, the bandleader, asked about 15 times. "Why don't you consider something more traditional, like 'That's Amore?'"

It turned out everything he sang – even Kool & the Gang's "Celebration" – somehow sounded like "That's Amore." We could only laugh and melt into one another's arms as he massacred "That's Amore" – er, "Handle With Care" – as we danced surrounded by a couple hundred friends and family.

Still, we wouldn't have picked any other song. There was never any question that it would be our first dance, just as there was no question as to where we'd go on our honeymoon: Liverpool.

Chapter 4: A Dip in Liverpool

It was more a lane than a street, flanked by brick slivers of houses, about 10 feet wide and not quite twice as tall. The neighborhood was, to use a local term, dodgy.

I was barely 24, but had been a reporter long enough to know what to do – get in, get what I needed and get the hell out.

So I pulled my point-and-shoot camera from its case and dashed in front of the tiny house on Admiral Grove in Liverpool's Dingle section, which never quite rebounded from the Blitz. I looked into the viewfinder, but didn't press the shutter – I was too close to capture much more than the doorway of No. 10. I ran across the narrow lane, into the areaway of the house directly opposite. I pressed my back against the front door, ready to click away when our tour guide approached and aimed her right index finger at me.

"People live here," she said. "Have some respect."

I pressed the shutter anyway. If she was going to be in the picture, so be it. I hadn't come all this way to miss a chance to photograph the house where Ringo was raised.

Back on the tour bus, Theresa and I had our first fight – or row, in the local argot – since getting married eight days earlier.

"You shouldn't have done that," she said. "What

could you have been thinking?"

"What's the big deal?" I asked. "We're never coming back here again, anyway."

"No. 1, that's not true," she sighed, shaking her head as if, correctly, she were talking to a pathetic fool. "No. 2, you embarrassed all of us."

She was referring to our good friends Julie and Graham. We were staying with them in Merseyside and they gamely accompanied us on the tour. Even their children – two-year-old Amanda, and Ryan, who was less than a month old – didn't appear pleased with me. Graham, a native Liverpudlian, looked particularly mortified. "I'm sorry," he told the guide. "He's from New York."

I wasn't sure what to expect a couple days earlier as our train pulled out of the cloudy English countryside into Lime Street Station. All I knew about Lime Street is that it had been the center of Liverpool's seedy district in years past ("And she'll never walk down Lime Street anymore," the Beatles sang in their version of "Maggie May," the traditional Liverpudlian ode to a wayward woman). Rain began falling as the train sighed to a halt in the station, a stop on the world's first passenger railway line. The vaulted steel-and-glass ceiling gave us – and a whole mess of hovering pigeons – cover from the drops as we looked for Graham. We quickly spotted him at the end of the platform.

"Welcome to Liverpool," he said. "The birthplace of a very important person – me."

Thirty seconds in Liverpool and we'd gotten our first dose of the local humor: wry and aimed at puncturing pretensions.

He grabbed the larger of our two black duffle bag-style suitcases and led us to his car parked outside. "Oh, have I got a surprise for you, Jere," he said. "We've got a big day planned tomorrow."

Great, I thought – maybe he'd booked a Beatles tour or would introduce us to some relative who knew them. I had done some research: Bus tours ran on the weekends, but not many of them. We weren't able to reserve spots ahead of time, at least not from overseas. I was determined to be on that first bus in the morning. The tour, aside from reconnecting with good friends (Theresa and I had worked at the accounting firm with Julie), was what we came here for, after all.

Graham couldn't contain himself. Standing in front of his car, he reached into his pants pocket and pulled out two red tickets. "I've got us seats to Liverpool versus Aston Villa. This is a big match!" he gushed.

"Great!" I said, forcing a smile. I love sports, though I held no affinity for soccer. As a seven-year-old, I played on a school team that was an exercise in misery – endless laps, forward and backward, which I hated running in either direction. The team was made up of boys ages six to 13, meaning I barely got to play in games – and when I did, the seventh and eighth graders trampled me. We'd spend half the practices looking for the coach, whom we'd inevitably find in the local bar watching the Mets on their amazing "Ya-Gotta-Believe" 1973 pennant run. Those were the games I was interested in, not soccer, which Graham and the rest of the non-U.S. world insisted on calling "football."

What did soccer have to do with the Beatles? Sure, Albert Stubbins, a player on the Liverpool team during their early boyhood made the cover of "Sgt. Pepper's Lonely Heart's Club Band." And they gave Matt Busby, who played for Liverpool in the 1930s but was better known for later managing archenemy Manchester United, a shout out in "Dig It." Still, the Beatles weren't big sports guys. "There are three teams in Liverpool and I prefer the other one," George once quipped.

But "football," I quickly gathered from Graham's excitement and from the red Liverpool jerseys and blue Everton shirts worn by men pouring out of pubs on Lime Street, was everything in this city. Certainly a lot more important than some defunct pop group.

After finding Graham's car, we picked up a dinner of fish and chips – and Chinese food – from the local chippie, and brought it back to his and Julie's home. To get us in a local state of mind, Graham rented "Shirley Valentine," about a Liverpool housewife who embarks on an overseas adventure.

Later, as we settled into our honeymoon suite – a mattress that took up most of the floor of the tiny living room – I turned to Theresa. "Do I have to go to this game?" I asked. "How do I get out of this? When are we going to get to go on the Beatles tour? What if we miss it? What if they don't have them on Sundays? What if it's too crowded and we don't get on the bus? What if there's some holiday we don't know about and all the tours are canceled?"

"You're going to the game," she said. "Didn't you see how excited Graham is? Don't worry. You worry too much. Try to relax and have fun for once."

We started the next day at Mathew Street, the site of the Cavern Club, where the Beatles became Liverpool stars. The club closed in the early 1970s and the building was knocked down. The Cavern was rebuilt across the street in the mid-1980s, purportedly using the original bricks, but was shuttered again about a year before our visit, presumably because of a lack of business.

We dropped into the Beatles Shop, then a modest memorabilia store, and went to the Beatles Story, a new, sparsely outfitted museum at Liverpool's Albert Docks, once a center of world shipping, now home to a mini-mall. But besides the museum, a couple stores and a decidedly odd 1970s statue affixed to a Mathew Street wall depicting the Beatles with the Madonna (Jesus' mom, not that material girl from Detroit), there wasn't a lot of evidence of the city's most famous sons.

Many Liverpudlians, we learned, felt that John, Paul, George and Ringo had forsaken their hometown after hitting the big time, leaving behind a bitter mix of anger and pride. According to vastly exaggerated local legend, a Beatle hadn't stepped foot into Liverpool since 1965. As a middle-aged woman we met on the train up to Liverpool put it, "They forgot us, so we forgot them."

As anxious as I was to see some historic Beatle

sites, Graham was even more eager to get to the game. In the early afternoon, we left the women and children in Liverpool's City Centre mall and hopped a cab to Anfield, home of the Liverpool Football Club.

We exited into a swarm of men, red-faced and shouting, spilling out of the bars that seemed to ring the stadium in concentric circles. Graham looked at his watch. It was about 15 minutes to game time. "What do you think, Jere?" he asked, a mischievous smile curling up his thin moustache. "Do you want to grab a quick one?"

"Can't we just get a beer inside?" I asked.

Graham laughed. "Oh, they don't sell beer in there. It's against the law."

So we swam against the boozy tide into the closest pub, got a pint each and downed them in a couple of gulps. We joined the flow of bodies into the gates of the century-old stone stadium, riding a current of electricity that I'd only felt before at the 1986 World Series at Shea Stadium. But a greater sense of danger lurked here. Slightly buzzed (I was buzzed, anyway), we stumbled up to our seats. I wasn't struck by the perfect green pitch as much as by the cacophonic roar. Groups in different sections were shouting and singing at one another, in a vicious call-and-response.

> *Who the fuck, who the fuck,*
> *Who the fucking hell are you!*
> *Who the fucking hell are you!*
> *Li-ver-pool, Li-ver-pool,*
> *Li-ver-pool, Li-ver-pool*

Much of the yelling was directed at one grandstand, which was fenced off, behind one of the goals. Some fans tried to scale the fence, only to be pulled down and clubbed by police.

"What's that all about?" I asked.

"That's where the Aston Villa supporters stand," Graham said.

"They separate the fans?"

"Yeah," he said. "They want to prevent fights. They're a lot stricter since Hillsborough."

I didn't know much about soccer, but I knew about Hillsborough. About a year and a half earlier, nearly 100 Liverpool supporters attending a game in Sheffield were trampled to death in a human stampede.

I looked around for the closest exit, just in case.

The din grew louder as the match unfolded. I'd been to Game 6 of the 1986 World Series, when it felt like Shea Stadium was going to collapse under me after Mookie Wilson's bouncer scooted through Bill Buckner's legs. Bleacher Creatures pelted me with garbage at Yankee Stadium when I cheered Tom Seaver's 300th career victory against the Bombers in 1985. I'd avoided injury in Madison Square Garden's old blue seats during brawls at Ranger-Islander games.

But I'd never experienced a sporting event as frightening – or as exhilarating – as this. Aston Villa scored the first goal. I arrived not caring who won. But suddenly, I had a vested interest in rooting for Liverpool. If Liverpool were to lose, things could turn ugly.

Luckily, Liverpool came back and scored before the end of the half. I could live with – or, more to the point, survive – a tie. But not the Liverpool or Aston Villa fans. The mania grew as time shortened, with more eyes trained at some points on the occasional blur of fists in the stands than on the footwork on the field. The dueling singsong chants collided, like two fronts, boding a storming.

> *Who the fuck, who the fuck,*
> *Who the fucking hell are you!*
> *Who the fucking hell are you!*
> *Li-ver-pool, Li-ver-pool,*
> *Li-ver-pool, Li-ver-pool*

With a couple minutes left, Liverpool scored, setting off a frenzy about three-quarters jubilation, one-quarter misery. We already were making our way to the aisle as the clock ran out and the crowd erupted. As the throng sang, "You'll Never Walk Alone," the Rogers and Hammerstein classic later covered by Gerry and the Pacemakers and co-opted as the Liverpool team song, we pounded down the concrete stairs.

"How are we going to get back?" I asked.

"Don't worry," Graham said. "We'll just grab a bus."

A group of happily drunk men and boys already had grabbed a bus – and were shaking it.

"On second thought," Graham said, "maybe we'll just walk."

"Just watch yourself," he said. "It's a little dodgy. It's not as safe as New York."

New York in 1990 was far from a safe place – it was hurtling toward what would become the deadliest year in the city's history (not counting 9/11). In fact, the next day, a 22-year-old tourist from Utah named Brian Watkins, in town for the U.S. Open, would be stabbed to death on a Manhattan subway platform while defending his mother from a band of thugs. The crime made international headlines ("The Rotting of the Big Apple," Time magazine declared), focusing on unwanted spotlight on New York as the urban murder capital of the world.

I grew up in Brooklyn, and largely had avoided trouble in my 24 years. Graham, about four years older than I, had spent much of his twenties in New York and knew his way around some bad neighborhoods. So I heeded his words as we embarked on the winding three-mile walk through rows of tiny, attached council houses.

Kids kicked threadbare soccer balls through the narrow streets, while those barely out of childhood lurked on corners, smoking cigarettes, drinking cans of beer clumsily cloaked in paper bags. I did my New York thing of looking directly at no one, while soaking it all in and watching my back. These were the kind of streets the Beatles traversed as children and young men, in times of even greater deprivation, after World War II. If I wanted a real Beatle experience, I was getting it – in a way I'd never imagined.

We made it, unscathed, back to the City Centre, where we found Julie, Theresa and the children. "So, you had a good time," Theresa said, seeing from my wide grin there was no need to ask.

I needn't have worried about being at the end of the line for the tour bus the next day. There were so few folks queued they nearly canceled the tour, until a couple of German visitors bought tickets at the last minute. We climbed on the bus, which looked like it wouldn't make it around the block, forget about the city, and settled into our seats. The guide, a stout 40-ish woman, pressed the play button on a circa-1975 Sony tape recorder badly in need of new batteries.

"Rooooooolllll upppppp. Rooooooolllll upppppp foooorrr the myssssstery tourrrr," the tape dragged, like a 45 rpm record playing at 33 1/3.

She clicked off the tape, and gave a brief introductory spiel. Then she pressed play again before sitting down. "The magicaaalll myssssstery tourrrr is comingggg to taaaake youuuuu awaaaayyy," Paul sang, sounding like Barry White on downers.

So it went as we ventured into the Beatles' Liverpool. We stopped briefly at Penny Lane – we saw the roundabout, even if the shelter in the middle was long gone. We managed to dash out at Strawberry Field, and take a couple of pictures in front of the iron gates and stone walls marked with the name of the old Salvation Army orphanage where John strolled as a youngster. We made a loop from John's house to Paul's house to George's and Ringo's, where I made a fool of myself during my photo opportunity. As slow as the "Magical Mystery Tour" tape was, our tour flew by, running not much more than an hour.

It wasn't quite what I expected. I was part thrilled, part relieved and maybe just a tad disappointed. We stood outside a few places, but didn't get to enter any, and were quickly rushed back on the bus after each stop. And I didn't much like getting yelled at – even if I deserved it.

As we boarded the train the next morning at Lime Street station, still arguing about my paparazzi follies, I focused on Theresa's reaction to my remark that we'd never be back here again. She didn't say it, but she seemed almost more disappointed with my lack of vision for our future than with my bad behavior. I was a kid who'd never traveled overseas until now, and feared this might be as good as things get. We were newly married and beginning to build a life. We would have many more adventures together. We'd just have to work hard to make them happen.

She was right, I decided, as the train pulled away: We would return someday.

Chapter 5: Our Beatle Baby

The nurse somehow managed to count her toes and fingers amid the kicking and punching, then swaddled her tight and placed her into my arms. I cradled her gently, but feared she would somehow leap onto the dull-white linoleum operating room floor and run out through the swinging double doors. She wasn't crying as much as growling. Her head shook as if she wanted to scream, "No! No! No!" I could feel her arms and legs trying to thump their way out from under her white, blue-striped terrycloth straitjacket.

I should have been elated, but felt helpless as I sat in the stiff-backed, cold metal chair shortly after 6 a.m. on that early March morning in 1997. Theresa lay prone on a gurney next to me, her lower half blocked by a sheet as the doctors stitched her up after an emergency cesarean section (I peeked – once. Someone should have warned me that love means never having to see your spouse's intestines). Tears dribbled down her pale cheeks as she dopily begged, "Let me see her."

I held up the wriggling bundle, terrified I would lose my grip. At eight pounds of flesh and bones topped by about 2 ¼ ounces of wispy light brown hair, this was both the smallest and most powerful human I had met in all my 30 years. I clasped her tight to my chest and began rocking forward and back, as if davening in prayer. But that somehow only made the screaming seem – and feel – louder, like a motorcycle revving atop me.

I pulled my face to close to hers, if only because I didn't want the doctor and nurses to see me cry tears of frustration over my inability to sooth my newborn daughter. I opened my mouth, and instead of the guttural pre-waterworks moan I feared, something resembling music spilled out: "Dum-dum-*dum-dum*. Dum-dum-dum-*dum-dum*.Dum-dum-dum-*dum-dum*. Dum-dum-dum-dum-dum (pause) *dum-dum-dum.*"

The crying stopped. So did the shaking. She cocked her head toward me. I saw her eyes for the first time – they were a steely, gray blue (where the hell did those come from? Theresa and I have brown eyes – so does the UPS guy). Her eyes seemed to ask: *Do I know you, sir?*

So I launched into my nonsense syllables again, but it wasn't a nonsense song. As Theresa's belly inflated to pink beach-ball proportions over the previous nine months, I occasionally performed my off-key version of "Love Me Do," my face as close to her stomach as it was now to the suddenly quiet little person in front of me, the one we decided to call Ella after a woman who could turn nonsense syllables into glorious music.

Why I picked that song, I can't say. There's something appealingly simple about the Beatle's first hit, and it's perhaps the easiest of their songs to play. The structure echoes a nursery rhyme. But that's over-thinking things after the fact – I went on pure instinct. I didn't realize it then, but that musical moment marked the first sign we would be raising a Beatle baby.

Not that we planned on having a Beatle baby –
any baby would have been fine by us. Theresa became
pregnant for the first time, very unexpectedly in 1992,
after about a year and a half of marriage. Panic gave
way to joy, which gave way to relief a short time later
when I landed a reporting job at the New York Daily
News for almost double the salary of my gig as editor
of Downtown Express, a weekly Lower Manhattan paper.

But just days before I started my dream job,
Theresa suffered a miscarriage – the first of four in
three years. During this period, Theresa's brother
Frankie died just shy of his 28th birthday. Her father,
John, who had triumphed over throat cancer shortly
before our wedding, started smoking again after losing Frankie, and passed away 11 months later. Amid all
this, we bought a house we couldn't afford and toiled
long hours to pay the bills, rarely seeing one another. I
worked on some of the biggest, if not always most important, stories of the time, including the O.J. Simpson
case. I was making a decent enough name for myself
as a reporter, but not as a husband as Theresa spent too
many nights alone, mourning too many losses.

We refused to get our hopes up when Theresa
learned she was pregnant a fifth time, not long after
her 34th birthday. Theresa suffered morning sickness
so severe that she began bringing a pillow into the
bathroom to nap on the cold tile floor between puking
bouts. She was bedridden for much of the pregnancy,
working on scripts and watching TV, as the child inside her never stopped kicking. "Maybe it'll be a drum-

mer," she'd joke. "We'll call it 'Ringo.'"

About eight months after "it" became "Ella," I transitioned into a gig as an editor. The hours were long, but at least more predictable, and the money was better. The responsibility was greater, just as it was at home. Besides a cranky infant who refused to sleep through the night for the first 18 months of her life, we cared for a century-old house that cried out for constant attention, leaving us in a never-ending nor'easter of baby tears, construction dust and loan documents.

When Ella was about three months old, Theresa returned to her part-time job at a Manhattan fashion photography studio so chi-chi that nobody seemed to notice it was housed in a dingy former garage. So this was our life: I'd stumble home around midnight, feed and rock Ella as needed. Theresa would leave for work at 6 a.m. I'd sleepwalk through the morning, eventually pack up Ella, drop her off with Theresa at about 1:30 p.m. and head to the Daily News.

The only times Ella wasn't crying was when she was eating (a family trait, to be sure), on the subway (a city girl from the start, naturally) or being serenaded.

For Theresa, whose weapons of woo include her beautiful voice, this meant constant singing. For me, it meant strumming tunes on my guitar, sometimes falling asleep mid-song – or just flipping on a CD and trying to sneak a few winks on the couch until Ella's next crying jag.

I became convinced, as the months passed, that Ella's constant crankiness stemmed from frustration at not being able to order us around. Nonsense sentences we didn't know how to answer were followed by withering stares that declared, "You're an idiot!" (It's a look she picked up from her mother). At six months or so, Ella began singing along with our efforts to soothe her, cooing to the music, sometimes remarkably in key. She was an early walker (she took her first steps at nine months and began running the next day), and talker. No, her first word wasn't "Ringo" (it was "Daddy," thank you very much), but her first stab at a sentence was Beatles related.

Our daily ritual included lunch, which consisted of Ella spitting, and later throwing, a rainbow of Gerber offerings at me, turning my ties into Jackson Pollock-like creations. She liked mashed banana and sweet potatoes, but hated peas – even if she smiled and clapped as Theresa and I sang, "All we are saying, is give peas a chance!"

Ella and my lunch would begin with legendary New York disk jockey Scott Muni, an early U.S. supporter of the Beatles, who kicked off his noon weekday show with four of the group's songs.

One afternoon, Muni, variously known as Scotso and The Professor, played "Love Me Do." Ella snatched the feeding spoon from my hand, and instead of hurling it at me as usual, turned in her booster seat and pointed the utensil at the silver boom box on the kitchen counter behind us. "Daddy's music!" she exclaimed, apparently stunned that it was emanating from the magic box, and not from my mouth or guitar.

"Yeah, Daddy wishes," I said.

Okay, so it wasn't technically a sentence (no verb). But as far as first phrases, "Daddy's music!" wasn't bad. She had made a connection, associating the Beatles with our family.

When Ella was 2 ½, we embarked on our first real trip in about six years, taking Theresa's mother for a first-ever visit to her family's ancestral home in Italy after spending a couple days in London. As we rolled Ella through Westminster, she pointed to Big Ben and yelled, "Mary Poppins!" recalling the opening scene from her then-favorite movie.

We, of course, took her on a Beatles walking tour, with the requisite pictures of us strolling across Abbey Road. It was less a stroll, though, than a mad dash, thanks to the unforgiving motorists for whom the tourist ritual is more annoying than charming.

By now, Ella had an inkling of who the Beatles were, if from nothing else than repeated viewings of "Yellow Submarine." But a full grasp eluded her. (When Ella was nearing four, we took a tour of Ben Franklin's home in Philadelphia, and the guide mentioned his time in Britain. "Did Ben Franklin meet the Beatles when he was in England?" Ella asked.)

We made a giant step – or rather, roll – toward taking the Beatles from the abstract to the concrete – as in sidewalk – in early August, 2001, when we learned Ringo would be playing a "Today" show mini-concert in Rockefeller Plaza.

Theresa and I already had bought tickets to see Ringo and the latest incarnation of his All-Starr Band later that month at the Garden State Arts Center in New Jersey, and made the tough decision to leave Ella home. Dragging a four-year-old across state lines to an amphitheater during a sweltering August did not sound like a good time for any of us, even if it was a rare opportunity– and possibly Ella's only chance, because you never know – to see a Beatle.

The "Today" show gig seemed like a good compromise, even if there were many things that could go wrong. We'd have to leave the house and get on the subway no later than 5 a.m. if we were to have a shot at getting onto the plaza. The show began at 7 a.m., and Ringo wouldn't go on until for at least an hour. Die-hard fans, I was positive, would be lining up the night before. We'd also have to mess with Ella's head a bit. Thankfully, she already was potty trained, but now we had to convince her to return to pull-ups and shed her "big-girl" underwear, at least for the day.

Even worse, after weaning her off her stroller, we had to strap her in for one last marathon ride, imprisoned behind Velcro straps. We needed to make sure we carried enough water, snacks and suntan lotion (not only for Ella, but for my balding head). We would not be traveling light.

Our biggest challenge, though, would be getting onto the plaza. Failure, which would have been crushing, was not an option.

Ella, at least in theory, was excited about this adventure. Getting her up and dressed at 4:30 a.m. provoked a different type of excitement. Getting me up and dressed on about three hours sleep proved even tougher. "Why don't we just forget about it?" I moaned, pulling my pillow over my head. "We're never going to get in anyway. There are people who probably have been sleeping there a week. Do you know what they're going to smell like in August?"

"Nobody is that crazy," Theresa said, yanking the pillow away. "And there probably aren't many people as crazy as us. You promised her. So get your lazy ass out of bed."

Lampposts lighted our path as we entered the subway station on our corner around 5 a.m. My back strained as I carried Ella, in her stroller, down the stairs – going up would be harder. At 35, I was getting too damn old for this. There was the requisite griping, re-criminations and assigning of blame. ("Why are we doing this?" "It was your idea." "No, it was you idea." "You promised." "I'm hungry." "I've got to pee." "Well, you should have thought about that before." "At least she has a diaper.")

Things brightened as we emerged from the subway at about 6 a.m., just as the sun rose over Manhattan. We raced down 48th Street to Rockefeller Plaza, which, while teeming, wasn't impenetrable. The stroller proved our salvation as we nudged our way into the crowd of polite out-of-towners and New Yorkers, who, no matter how brusque the reputation, usually will make way for a kid on wheels (at least after you roll over their feet).

We managed to make our way to within about 100 feet of the stage set up near the northern edge of the plaza – the overnight campers had the best spots, of course. Now all we had to do was wait – and keep Ella entertained. It wasn't difficult. She had seen the "Today" show enough times to get a kick out of the visitors waving their signs outside the studio windows – "Omaha Loves Matt!" "It's My Birthday!" "Kiss Me, Al!"

The usual band of tourists was joined by Beatles fans, who passed the time with impromptu sing-alongs. Staying still for Ella, as always, proved a challenge. But music kept her happy, and a year in pre-school had done wonders for her curiosity and attention span. Maybe it was a mistake not to buy her a ticket for that concert...

Once the show got underway, Matt Lauer worked the crowd, keeping up the energy and building the anticipation, leading to the eruption that greeted Ringo as he took the stage. When he launched into "Yellow Submarine," Ella no longer was one of the few children among the masses – we all were kids, transported to a shared moment in time, singing along, and stomping and waving our hands in unison, turning the plaza into a rolling sea of joy.

We were ready to declare victory and leave, even if Ringo was set to return in about an hour to close out the show. But when we turned around, there was nowhere to go: The crowd not only filled the plaza, but spilled onto 48th Street behind us, snarling what by now was rush-hour traffic. We all were past our limit. The morning sun turned from preheat to broil and Ella became understandably agitated. But we were stuck.

We were terrified she would cause a scene, and

saw the signs of impending meltdown ("I want to go – now!"). Luckily, some of the many moms and dads around us stepped in and helped keep Ella's attention off leaving ("What a lucky girl!" "I wish my son was here." "What a big girl you are!"). So we got by with a little help from some new friends, until Ringo returned to sing, "With a Little Help From My Friends."

We rolled home happy and watched the show on video, where there's a nanosecond glimpse of Ella during "Yellow Submarine" that I later accidentally taped over (with a Paul special). For days, Ella told any-one who would listen, "I saw Ringo!"

Chapter 6: The Gardener of Friar Park

It was through the "Today" show, just over a month after our Ringo adventure, that I learned the second jet had struck the South Tower. About a half-hour earlier, I had dropped Ella off at her pre-school – it would be the first time she would spend a full day there, and we had packed her off with lunch and lectures. "When the teacher says it's nap time, you need to go to sleep," Theresa told her.

"Or at least close your eyes and pretend," I said, getting a laugh from Ella and a smirk from Theresa.

On the way back from voting in the New York City mayoral primary election, I spotted a small crowd gathered around a parked car with the radio blaring. A small plane or a helicopter – something – had hit the World Trade Center. I dashed home, and turned on the TV moments after the second plane hit. This clearly was no accident. I grabbed a plastic shopping bag, tossed in some underwear, socks and toiletries, and bolted out the door for the subway.

The next few weeks remain a blur, but I do know we were blessed not to lose any family or other loved ones, despite some close calls. Many dear to us weren't spared that agony. So much happened at work, but it's the moments at home I remember most. I decided that no matter what, I wouldn't be staying in a hotel near my Manhattan office, though that would have been the smart thing to do, at least professionally. I needed to make a daily appearance at home to maintain some semblance of normalcy, even if in the first few days after the tragedy my pit stop consisted of little more than a couple hours sleep and a shower.

Ella knew what happened, though she, like the rest of us, couldn't understand it. Many friends didn't talk about the attacks or put on the TV in front of their kids for weeks. We left the TV on and didn't watch what we said. It was all around us, after all: the candles on the stoops; the American flags hanging from the homes, including ours; the passersby with the haunted faces; the mournful skirl of bagpipes heralding yet another funeral in one of the local churches; the black bunting draped across firehouses fronted by moats of flowers and candles.

The world had changed in a few terrifying instants. But I knew that no matter what my work duties, I needed to be there when Ella woke up – or, more often, when she woke me up. "Here, Daddy," she said, as she nudged me awake the morning of Sept. 13. "Give this to your friends to make them feel better."

I shook the sleep from my eyes and looked on the pillow next to me. She had left her foam, toy mask of a firefighter's smiling face.

That morning, we attempted to drive Ella to pre-school, but traffic wasn't moving. We were stuck atop a hill, a block from our house, looking down at what we later determined was the waterfront smokestack whose white-smoke belches we somehow never noticed before. "Oh, that's not good, that can't be good," Theresa said, panic creeping into her voice.

"It's nothing," I said. "Fires generate black

smoke. The only thing white smoke means is that a new pope's been elected."

"Maybe the World Trade Center blew up again," Ella piped in with a chilling matter of factness.

As the world got crazier, with the November crash of Flight 587 in a Queens neighborhood of row houses that looked a lot like ours, the war unfolding in Afghanistan, and anthrax being mailed to news or-ganizations (it wasn't exactly reassuring to see feds in spaceman-like suits walk into the Daily News' mail-room), the stress built.

Ella began screaming in her sleep. But wak-ing up didn't stop the images – a couple of times, her nightmares continued with her gray-blue eyes wide open. We held her as Theresa would sing her, not back to sleep, but into better dreams with a soothing, lullaby whisper: "Golden slumbers fill Ella's eyes."

About five weeks after the attacks, I spent my first full daddy-daughter day with Ella, who had picked up an odd habit of clinging to scraps of paper and other detritus, saying she needed them for unspecified "art projects." After lunch and ice cream with friends about a mile from home, we called it a day. We missed the bus. She wouldn't walk, so I carried her. She also in-sisted that I lug the wrapper from her ice cream cone, and the paper plate that had held her hot dog.

My back ached under my burden, which in-cluded guilt that I had spent so little time lately with Ella and my growing concern about her post-9/11 gar-bage-collecting mania. About a block from our house, I could take no more – I placed her down and told her she had to walk. Then I slam-dunked the trash in an overstuffed corner wastebasket.

As I bent down to talk to her, she grabbed my neck with both hands, scratched my face, bit my ear, and called me "a littler fucker." That shocked me – Theresa and I didn't generally watch our language, but I'm not sure where she heard that one. (The only time she ever cursed before was at age 2 when she indignantly called me a "big in-the-ass pain.")

I was still shaken by her outburst the next night when we gathered around the TV to watch the Concert For New York City, the benefit at Madison Square Garden put together by Paul, who frequently visited rescue workers after the tragedy. We awoke Ella for his set, which closed the show and included a new song, "Freedom," inspired by the attacks.

It marked the first time Ella had seen Paul perform live, even if only on TV. "He looks different than in 'Hard Day's Night,'" she said, her brow knitted in concern. "Is he okay? I think he's older now."

There were rumors before the show that the three surviving Beatles would reunite – if any cause could bring them together, this would seem to fit the bill. But I knew by then, thanks to our intrepid reporters, George was in no shape to appear.

I volunteered in October to start preparing his obituary, and got no argument from my exhausted bosses. With everything going on in the world, the fate of one man – even one known and beloved around the world – seemed insignificant. It was less a professional fear of being caught unprepared that drove me than a sense of duty.

I gathered clips folder – a dozen or more small manila pouches stuffed with hundreds of yellowing newspaper stories mentioning George from the days of Beatlemania through the bizarre stabbing attack in his home by a crazed man in late 1999, just before the millennium. I stayed late one night, and wrote a quick just-in-case draft. In the coming days, I'd frequently return to the obituary and spiff up the prose, adding a paragraph or two more – there was much to tell.

The exercise seemed morbid, especially with the news dominated for weeks by death. Even as TV resumed regular programming, there was a feeling that the popular culture had changed with the country. The late-night hosts were subdued. Articles appeared declaring an end to irony (whatever that meant), and predicting a future with less emphasis on entertainment and frivolity. My gut told me that soon enough people would crave diversion more than ever.

Theresa woke me up early on Nov. 30 to tell me George had died. My first instinct was to find out what time the news broke, to see if the story had made any of the papers. It turned out he passed away the day before, but his family held back on an announcement until that morning. We wouldn't be breaking news, but we'd have an opportunity to give readers a full picture as possible of not just George's death, but more importantly, of his life.

It was a Friday, my normal day off, but I called to say I would be in. The bosses – editor-in-chief Ed Kosner and executive editor Michael Goodwin, who had led us through the past 11 weeks of insanity – boldly decided we'd put out a special 12-page section to wrap around the paper, filled with sidebars and photographs. I polished the obituary, adding details and quotes from Ringo and Paul, who said, "He is really, just my baby brother."

A team of weary reporters and editors banded to produce a beautiful tribute, even if in the greater scheme of things there was more important news to worry about.

An early start meant an early finish. I arranged to meet Ella and Theresa at the one place we knew Beatle fans would be: Strawberry Fields in Central Park. As I entered at nightfall, strains of "Here Comes the Sun" greeted me as the wind whipped through the park, lit by scores of candles carried by the crowd. The only ones, it seemed, who weren't clutching candles were those strumming guitars or banging tambourines.

Unlike past vigils there, there was a sense of almost relief, the kind of burden excising exhale we experience when a loved one is released from suffering. Faces etched for weeks with grief now seemed almost serene.

Perhaps it helped that many children were among the throng. As the sing-along moved into "Can't Buy Me Love," Ella and I found a free patch of grass, and ran about goofily like the Beatles did in that wonderful scene in "A Hard Day's Night," when they escape the demands of fame for a few precious minutes of carefree lunacy. (The movie was a favorite of Ella's, who would bar us from the living room, close the doors and run up and down the cherry-wood floor, screaming with the rest of the crazed fans in the opening sequence.)

The next day, the three us looked through all the newspapers together. Ella, three months from her fifth birthday, was just starting to read. One word jumped out at her: "Hester! That's us!" It was my first byline since Ella was an infant. I felt a strange pride in her discovery, and I could see in her bright eyes the special connection she felt to the story.

About a week later, Theresa struck up a conversation about George with Julia, the mother of one of Ella's pre-school classmates. It turned out Julia had been raised in Henley-on-Thames, the town where George lived in Friar Park, a rambling estate with a castle built by a local rich eccentric (saluted in song by George in "The Ballad of Sir Frankie Crisp"). Friar Park was George's refuge from the world, a sanctuary where he indulged in his love of gardening.

Julia told Theresa and Ella how she sometimes ran into George at the local pub, once finding him alone in the kitchen, fixing himself a sandwich.

Ella became fascinated by Julia's sweet childhood memories of George. She demanded I tell her more about Friar Park. I pulled out some books from our ample Beatles library, showed her pictures of George's Gothic, whimsically inviting home and read a few passages aloud. "We," she announced, "are going to write a song about George's castle."

She handed me a pen and paper, and began to dictate her list of what should be in the song. "We have to mention his garden. We have to say it's a castle! We need to talk about the big gates in front."

I started to draft lyrics that she was quick to critique. "I don't know what that means – make it simpler," she'd say – sounding just like a newspaper editor.

The George-inspired tune I crafted in the ensuing days proved tougher to negotiate. "I don't like that part – make it more like this," she'd say. Then she'd sing a phrase. It took a few weeks, but this is what we came up with:

> *Well I ran into a friend who used to live in Henley*
> *And she knew someone we all know, but not in the same way*
> *He was the gardener in the castle, at the Friar Park estate*
> *And people would come from the world around*
> *Just to peek through the iron gates*
>
> *There were gnomes and caves and passages that wound through the grounds*
> *There were topiaries and wishing wells and even pythons to be found*
>
> *As he tilled the soil, the gardener would tend to matters of the soul*
> *Chant his mantra, play his ukulele, but he could still rock and roll*
> *Along with his flowers, the gardener raised a son,*
> *And sometimes he'd slip away to the pub when his work was done*

Even as his body was ailing,
His garden was desecrated by a sword
Though he'd plant another season
He would soon meet his Sweet Lord

It was a cold November morning when we learned
that George had died
So we went to Strawberry Fields, sang
some songs and we cried
There we ran into our friend who knew him all
those years ago
And she spoke of his Crackerbox Palace and the
seeds that he sowed
As our candles cut a beam across the New York
autumn dark
Back in that pub in Henley they lifted a glass to
the gardener of Friar Park

"It's good," Ella said. "But take out 'topiaries.'"

"Nope," I said. " 'Topiaries' stays."

It became clear to Theresa and me that the song was Ella's way of trying to take control of and make sense of all the death that surrounded us during those dark weeks. You could do worse with pain and confusion, I supposed, than turning it into art and a celebration of a life.

Not long after we finished she song, Ella declared, "I want to go there."

"Where?" I asked.

"To George's castle."

"Maybe some day, Ella. Maybe some day."

Chapter 7 : Birthday

The kids' non-stop shrieks of laughter threatened to shatter my eardrums. Which came as a relief. We didn't know how the 15 or so kindergarteners – and twice as many parents – packed into our living room would react to Bob Abadou, aka Mr. Puppet, who is the world's premiere (and possibly only) Beatles puppeteer. Theresa and I hired Bob to perform at Ella's sixth birthday celebration, which, at her request, was Beatle-themed. While we took a certain perverse pride in her party wishes, her desire for a Beatles bash added to our growing concern about the little Fab Four-headed monster we had created.

Ella's kindergarten attire alternated between a pair of pink T-shirts emblazoned with "The Beatles" and a blue T-shirt plastered with the "A Hard Day's Night" album cover (original British version, of course). The shirts earned Ella some teasing in school ("Hey, here comes Beatles girl!"). Her insistence on making her friends watch "A Hard Day's Night" on play dates also threatened to establish her a reputation as a bore (especially when she would rarely entertain her pals' compromise suggestions to watch the more kid-friendly "Yellow Submarine").

She proved equally stubborn in her musical selections, demanding all Beatles, all the time, while her friends wanted to hear Barney, Kidz Bop and Raffi. Much of this was our own fault: When Ella asked why we never played Radio Disney in the car like other parents, Theresa replied without hesitation: "Our radio doesn't get that station."

Ella accepted the explanation without question.

While Ella's quirks charmed most adults, her peers weren't quite as amused and we began to worry we were raising an obstinate outcast. As proud as we were of her strong sense of self, like any parents we wanted our child to fit in.

Some of our fears abated at the party as the kids entertained themselves by making tie-dye T-shirts, stringing groovy love bead necklaces and recording a group sing-along of "Yellow Submarine" using the small karaoke machine we had bought Ella for her birthday. But Bob's performance proved the day's biggest hit, as he trotted out his various Beatles puppets (two sets – one clad in circa-1964 garb, the other in Sgt. Pepper costumes). The Ringo puppet got the most laughs, via goofy Borsht Belt-style banter with Bob and kid's joke-book humor ("Ringo" explained why during a trip to the zoo he fed the elephant a $100 bill: "The sign said, 'Don't feed the elephant peanuts – $100 fine.'").

It wasn't an all-Beatle performance. Bob called me up to the front of the living room and declared that dads always get a special role in his shows. He wrapped a multi-color cape around my neck, placed a big black pompadour wig atop my balding head and handed me a toy guitar. Bob played a tape of "All Shook Up." I gamely lip-synched and wiggled my ample hips. I felt more than a little self-conscious – particularly because of my weight, which had ballooned by 40 pounds in my 11 years at the News, much of it gained in the busy 18 months since 9/11. "Thank you very much," I said in my best Elvis drawl when the song mercifully ended.

But my humiliation wasn't over: "Give a big hand to Elvis – the final days!" Bob declared.

Everybody laughed, which was fine – at least they weren't laughing at Ella.

We'd met Bob at The Fest for Beatles Fans, the one place it's guaranteed no one will ever laugh at you for loving John, Paul, George and Ringo. Mark Lapidos started what was initially called Beatlefest in 1974, using his life savings to book space in Manhattan's old Commodore Hotel. He received the blessing of John, who told him, "I'm all for it. I'm a Beatles fan, too!"

The Fest quickly grew, expanding to venues across the country. The annual three-day conventions now draw thousands of fans with sound-alike contests, trivia competitions and appearances by Beatle-linked journalists, actors, acts and intimates that have included Patti Boyd Harrison, Pete Best, Denny Laine, and Peter and Gordon. The Fests are the purest intergenerational celebration of all things Beatles, with the crowd ranging from those getting their first teeth to the dentures set. I've been going for more than 30 years, and teenagers consistently seem to be the largest group represented.

My first Fest experience came at age 15 in September 1981 as fans still reeled from the tragedy of 10 months earlier. I arrived looking for a place where I might fit in when I walked alone into the Penn Plaza

Hotel, across the street from Madison Square Garden. Glenn Miller immortalized the hotel's phone number in song ("Pennsylvania 6-5000!"), hitting the charts the week Ringo was born. By now the Penn Plaza, like many other New York landmarks from its era, was experiencing humbler times. I'd been to the hotel before for a couple of comic book/sci-fi fan conventions during the not-so-far-removed chubby pre-adolescent days when Spider-man and The Fantastic Four filled the gap between hide-and-seek and girls.

This wasn't a Trekker convention, not by a phaser shot. A surplus of would-be Johns, in wired-rimmed granny glasses, green army jackets and acoustic guitars slung across backs, bumped strings in the halls. I wore a green turtleneck sweater not all that different from the one John sported on the "Woman" single cover, though my clunky plastic glasses were more Woody Allen-like than Lennon vintage. One look-alike already was clad, stitch-for-stitch and cowboy hat, in the Western-inspired getup John wore on the cover of the just-released "Watching the Wheels" single.

I did a lot of watching myself: I kept my eyes glued to the fingers of the guitar players in the sound-alike contests, trying to pick up chords and licks. In darkened conference rooms, I saw footage I didn't know existed: the Beatles performing "Shout" on Swedish TV circa 1963, John and Yoko on "The Mike Douglas Show" in 1972, bootleg footage of John singing "Come Together" (adding the lyric "stop the war") during that year's "One to One" concert at Madison Square Garden. In the giant flea market area, I stared longingly at the T-shirts, posters, old Beatles toys (lots of very expensive copies of the Milton Bradley Beatles "Flip Your Wig" board game) and other memorabilia. I flipped through milk crates stuffed with various rock album imports and bootlegs, including one of John singing a song called "Serve Yourself," a Dylan spoof I wouldn't hear until its legitimate release nearly 20 years later.

I had a subway token to get home and barely enough cash for a hotdog and a soda, though I dipped into the "mugger money" in the back pocket of my brown corduroys to buy the least expensive cool item I could find: an Abbey Road street-sign keychain.

"I want to go there someday," I thought.

But the key chain, which cost a buck, might be the closest I'd ever get.

With Sony Betamaxes only just beginning to creep into living rooms (my family wouldn't get a VCR until 1984), fans packed into the main ballroom by the thousands to watch "A Hard Day's Night," "Help!," "Magical Mystery Tour," "Yellow Submarine" and "Let it Be," cheering wildly during the songs and favorite scenes. The films were rarely played on TV – in the wee hours, if at all – and surfaced occasionally at midnight movie showings I wasn't yet allowed to attend.

Over the years, I returned almost annually even as the Fest moved to the Meadowlands Hilton in New Jersey. As an early high school graduation present, my Aunt Rose took me in February 1984 to a special Beatle-fest dinner-concert, celebrating the 20th anniversary of the group's arrival in the U.S. Richie Havens played

"Here Comes the Sun." Phoebe Snow sang the hell out of "Don't Let Me Down." Tiny Tim offered a bizarre medley combining "All My Loving," "Tiptoe Through the Tulips" and "Imagine."

My highlight, though, was a men's room encounter with Harry Nilsson, the singer and songwriter best known for "Everybody's Talkin'" and "Without You." Harry, a pal of John's, became a Beatlefest fixture in the early 1980s, helping raise money to stop handgun violence. Sadly, he battled his own demons and was smashed as he wobbled toward the urinal next to mine. "You're a kid," he said in the strong Brooklyn accent than never deserted him, even after his singing voice crumbled under too many years of hard living. "What are you doin'? Why are you here?"

"For the Beatles," I said, softly, not averting my gaze from the business at hand. "And for John."

"John was the greatest, man," Nilsson said, stopping midstream and slapping my back. "I wish you coulda met him. He was the best. Give peace a chance, man. He said it all."

I left the men's room high in another way, not at all minding the splatter of Nilsson pee on my shoes.

I hooked Theresa on the Fest shortly after we started dating, and we introduced Ella to the scene around her fifth birthday. The Fest blew Ella's mind – the musicians, the music, the videos and the giant ballroom brimming with merchandise, including the T-shirts that would become her de-facto school uniform.

The Fest's offerings expanded every year, with

a Beatles "recording studio" eventually set up for fans to make karaoke cassettes of songs. Ella gravitated toward the room and belted out a strong version of "I Saw Her Standing There" that surprised Theresa and me. "She can really sing," said the recording engineer, who was equally impressed she could read all the lyrics on the prompter.

We happily accepted his kind words, though figured he said that to all the parents. As he made a copy of the cassette for us, we chatted and learned his day job was teaching music to elementary school students. He led Ella through some simple scales. "You might want to think about getting her some serious instruction when you think she's ready," he advised.

Ella already had gotten some music practice outside our home as a toddler when we started taking her to Music Together – an international program that offers family music classes led by specially trained teachers. The idea is to expose children to singing, tonal and rhythm patterns from infancy on, through sing-alongs and play-alongs using simple instruments like egg-shaped shakers and kid-sized drums.

Ella, to my horror, initially spent every class running up and down the room screaming, throwing instruments and generally terrorizing the other children and their caregivers to a mellow soundtrack that included "I've Been Working on the Railroad" and "When the Saints Come Marching in." I spent most of the sessions chasing her and apologizing in Hurricane Ella's wake. The teacher, Susan Hoffman, told me not to worry: "She's absorbing it all. She's interacting with music in her own way."

I thought it was a bunch of well-meaning, hippy-dippy nonsense.

But in the semesters to come, Ella began participating and developed a keen sense of rhythm and an uncanny ability to sing on key, even anticipating the next notes of songs she hadn't heard before. Music Together was great for Ella, and I saw an opportunity for Theresa, then chafing under unsatisfying part-time work. I encouraged her to look into putting her voice to use as a teacher. She went to Music Together's Princeton, N.J., headquarters for training, and soon started leading classes in our neighborhood. Just as Ella aged out of the program, Theresa got the opportunity to buy our local branch. We jumped at the chance, by then total Music Together converts.

Ella felt at home at Music Together – just as she did at The Fest. She seemed to strike a strong connection and sense of belonging amid the throngs of fans – especially the hundreds of kids who filled the main ballroom with laughter at Bob's Beatle puppet antics.

Ella talked about her first Fest for weeks. "I went to a Beatles concert in New Jersey!" she announced to the parents and kids at the bus stop as I took her to pre-school the Monday after our weekend adventure.

I gently told her later that we hadn't been to a Beatles concert – yes, we'd seen Ringo at the "Today" show some months before, but we'd never seen Paul in person – and of course, without John and George, there could be no Beatles.

She appeared lost in thought for a moment.

"Did your parents ever take you to a Beatles concert?" she asked.

"No," I replied. "The Beatles did their last concert in San Francisco when I was just a month old."

"That's no excuse," she said. "They should have gotten tickets and gone to San Francisco."

"My parents weren't Beatle fans," I responded, trying to keep a straight face. "I don't think they ever would have thought about taking me to a Beatles show."

"That's crazy," she said. "It's every parents' duty to take their children to see the Beatles! I'm going to have a talk with your mother about this!"

The very opinionated and spirited Ella was becoming her own person, even if she tended to see the world through the Beatle lenses we'd imposed on her. What other kid, after all, would request a Beatles puppet show for her birthday?

She was fitting in, in her own way. We could see she'd made some great friends as her little pals gathered after Bob's puppet show in our dining room to sing "Happy Birthday." Immediately after, the parents spontaneously burst into the Beatles' "Birthday" and I grabbed my guitar and followed along. This delighted Ella, even if most of her fellow kindergarteners were confused.

Theresa cut the cake – a vanilla sheet cake covered in an icing rendering of the "Hard Day's Night" album cover (again, the British version) with the 25 iconic headshots of the Beatles. Only in the middle, where George's head is turned away from the camera, we placed a small picture of a smiling Ella.

Bob came down for a piece of cake and to say goodbye. He handed me a couple of Polaroids he had taken of me in the Elvis get-up. God, was I fat. I put down my cake and picked up my guitar.

Chapter 8: Flying

I told Ella no – and not just because I didn't want to spend the two pounds, then worth about $3.50. That was far too much for a ride that would last 10 seconds, and probably cost far more in the long run for psychiatric bills to treat the trauma.

"You're not only a cheapskate, you're a killjoy," Theresa told me as she handed Ella a two-pound coin. "Go ahead, Ella. Daddy's outvoted."

I may have been outvoted, but I was right: The giant inflatable slide was by far the biggest of its kind that I'd ever seen, rising about 25 feet before unfurling like a dragon's puffy yellow tongue. This seemingly benign monster ride was dwarfed, though, by a backdrop of buildings lining the Liverpool waterfront – most prominently, the Royal Liver Insurance Building, topped by the two stone Liver birds, mythical creatures charged with overseeing the city of their birth and the River Mersey. (The birds' name rhyme with "diver," not "river" – go figure.)

We were nearing the end of the greatest vacation of our lives, during which Ella had grown more poised and confident seemingly with each moment. Though not quite eight-and-a-half, she impressed the fellow travelers on our 12-day "Magical History Tour" of London and Liverpool with her maturity, her Beatles knowledge, and, most of all, her endurance. She stayed up well past any normal child's (or adult's) bedtime to hang out in crowded clubs, listening to the umpteenth Beatles cover band, while generally regaining her fresh enthusiasm by the morning as we traveled in the often-obscure footprints of the group.

But this was her day – and all of Liverpool's. The city's annual Beatles Week is capped by a three-day end-of-summer holiday in which the City Centre is transformed into a giant street fair with rides, amusements and live music on a half-dozen stages scattered through the downtown. So Ella had an opportunity to be a kid, and part of that meant trudging up this giant inflatable slide.

Nothing would get in her way – except for a fear of heights, apparently inherited from the cheapskate killjoy. She climbed to the top without peeking down, sat, soaked in the view, froze like a statue and promptly began weeping.

Other kids simply pushed by her and slid down. The cranky operator wouldn't let me walk up the inflated stairs, so I took off my shoes and when he wasn't looking, started climbing up the slide to get her. That's something I'd never been able to do before my humiliation by Bob the puppeteer spurred the diet and exercise regimen that helped me lose 40 pounds by Ella's seventh birthday party. The mouthy Liverpool kids whizzed passed me laughing and cursing ("Fuck out of the way!" said one who was probably no more than seven). I didn't pay them much mind and I didn't look down.

I tried hard to never let my own fear of heights, which grew into a general fear of flying, get in the way

73

– no crippling Jimmy Stewart-"Vertigo"-like paralysis for me. On the rare occasions I needed to fly out of town on a reporting assignment, adrenaline and a different kind of anxiety – the subsuming fear of getting beat on the story – gave me wings.

But I was damn good about avoiding planes – "Who needs to travel when you live in New York?" I rationalized – even when it involved work. The first time the World Trade Center was attacked, in 1993, my bosses told me to join a photographer in a helicopter the paper had rented, so I could write a piece about the view from above the smoking North Tower. "Um, there probably won't be much to see other than smoke," I impoliticly hemmed and hawed, amid the deadline chaos of what was then the biggest story I'd ever worked on.

I generally was a good soldier who never turned down an assignment – including going undercover, variously, to take a bus filled with crackheads to an upstate homeless shelter and to drive a taxi at a time when cabbies were being slain at a rate of one a month. But those were joyrides, in my mind, compared to any helicopter jaunt. Luckily, a better soldier – a veteran reporter who had flown choppers in Vietnam – leaped at the chance for a return to the skies and I managed to save face.

Our last big family trip – at least one requiring getting on an airplane – came in 1999 when we visited England and Italy. Ella was 2 ½, and I lugged her car seat all over Europe, getting bemused looks from London cabbies and dirty looks from Rome hacks. But I was stubborn: I had read, somewhere on that relatively new phenomenon known as the World Wide Web, about a plane crash in which the only survivor was a child – strapped, of course, in a car seat.

After the particularly turbulent trip home, I resolved to stop getting on planes – and only became more determined when 9/11 provided another huge excuse. Exacerbating my fear wasn't terrorism, at least not directly: It was the realization that I was responsible for another life. How could I react in a crisis when mere taxiing was enough to make the blood drain from my white knuckles as my fingernails became one with the armrests?

I let my passport expire, if only to give me another out. In late 2002, though, I started to feel the gnaw of wanderlust with the announcement of "The Concert For George," which would be held in Royal Albert Hall, and feature Paul, Ringo, Eric Clapton and some of the Monty Python troupe. There was no way we'd be going. Even if we could get tickets, we couldn't afford the trip then or take the time off from work. It got me thinking, though: I couldn't let fear take away possibilities of opportunities – not just for me, but more importantly, for Ella. So I slowly warmed to the idea of a big Beatles adventure abroad.

On the plane ride to the UK, as excited as I was about our trip, I was my usual petrified self, trying not to breathe as we bounced across the Atlantic, with Ella, beyond her car seat years, nestled between Theresa and me. During one nasty bout of turbulence, I closed my eyes and turned up the music that pulsed through my headphones. "Hey Bulldog" came on. It's not on most lists of top Beatles songs, but it's one of my favorites, with its pounding piano riff, mad serpentine bass line and searing lead guitar with a John vocal to match. I tapped my right foot as if to steady the plane while John sang as if he were sitting next to me, advising me not to listen to my fears.

The turbulence suddenly calmed and so did I. I took that as a good sign and a message: I wasn't going to let my phobia interfere with our trip.

I felt only somewhat more secure as I trudged up the slide, my white-and-turning-grey tube socks losing the battle against gravity and the slippery rubber as I inched closer to the summit. But Ella's embarrassed whimpering, which grew louder as I ascended, drove me.

I reached the peak, smiled, if only for her sake, and turned around for a look. An unusually bright sun shined onto the River Mersey, while inland, a sea of people filled the Albert Docks and waterfront strip. From that height, the sounds of the different concerts and the murmur of the crowds wafted into one fairground-like mélange that would be our whirling soundtrack for the ride down.

I wriggled under Ella, placed her on my lap and wrapped my arms around her. "You know," I told her, "'Helter Skelter' is about a slide," as we pushed off and glided to the sidewalk under the protective gaze of the Liver birds.

Our journey back to Liverpool, began with, of

all people, Eric Clapton. In May 2004, Theresa and I went to see Slowhand at the Garden with my brother, Drew, and our close friend Diane Webber. Diane and her husband, Glenn Thrush, (they met at our first jobs in journalism, working for legendary editor Clay Felker at a small Manhattan newspaper called Downtown Express) were thinking about selling their Kensington co-op and buying a house elsewhere in Brooklyn.

As we waited for Clapton to take the stage, Theresa and Diane were leafing through a giveaway real estate ads rag when a man sitting behind us tapped Theresa on the shoulder. "Excuse me, are you looking for a house in Kensington?" he asked.

The mention of anything involving money was enough to make me bury my head back in my newspaper, but Theresa didn't miss a beat: "Whatcha got?"

A few days later, we walked into the lime-brick house on a quiet block about a mile and light years away from our perch in one of the hottest neighborhoods in the city. The dingy, but untouched woodwork – a rarity in neighborhood where Formica and paneling began a merciless march in the 1950s – drew our longing gaze. Then we turned to the dining room table, where several aunts, uncles, cousins and grandkids pored through an album of old pictures. It felt like home.

But home was a mess: holes in walls. Plaster chips dangling from the ceilings. And termites. Lots of them. Hungry enough and spritely enough to make it from the basement to the second floor. We needed to do a gut renovation – but were determined to restore and save every piece of wood the termites hadn't yet made a meal.

We were getting ahead of ourselves. The house was left to seven cousins by their late grandparents, but the deed was missing. The cousins were at odds over to whom to sell the house – a local contractor wanted to divide it into apartments; a real estate agent friend of the one cousins wanted a piece of the action. Most, though, were pulling for us – we hit it off with the folks we met at the Clapton concert and found that we all shared a love for the Beatles. "It's karma," they kept telling us. "You will get this house."

Meanwhile, we put our house in trendy Park Slope on the market at an outrageous price. It sold in a day. The deal to buy our termite-ridden dream home flicked on and off a half-dozen times, the victim of, variously, paperwork snags, disagreements among the cousins and ultimately, a bidding war.

Without a home to call our own, we moved the day before Thanksgiving 2004 into a sublet apartment above the flat shared by the landlady and her two Doberman pinchers, which kept a couple potentially homicidal neighbors at bay. We were bordering on homicidal ourselves, crammed into a bleak sublet, with most of our possessions in boxes or in storage. We had work to keep us busy – I had been promoted to city editor of the News a year earlier and Theresa, showing latent business acumen, had doubled the size of her Music Together branch.

After selling our house, we strutted like Rockefellers for a couple of days, sporting a bank balance so far into the black Chase called us in to confirm the deposit. But all we did was work and return to a place that wasn't home.

We were hopeful we'd someday buy the house we wanted, but even then we would be facing months of renovations to make it livable. We needed something to keep us going – more than karma.

A vacation, we decided, would do the trick. There was little discussion: We would take a tour of the Beatles' London and Liverpool, and this time we'd do it right. I'd been keeping up with changes in Liverpool over the years, if only in articles I'd read in magazines, on the news wires at work and online.

In the years after our 1990 honeymoon, Liverpool gradually re-embraced the Beatles – who cares about bad blood, when the all-you-need-is-love spirit is a ticket to ride on the gravy train? A Beatles industry, whose seeds were sown with the opening of Beatles Story shortly before our honeymoon and the second reopening of the Cavern Club a couple years later, finally boomed. It didn't hurt that Liverpool, like New York, had become a relatively safe place, at least according to the crime statistics. Paul had transformed the Liverpool Institute into a premier arts school and even had written a classical music ode to his hometown, "The Liverpool Oratorio." Yoko, we'd later learn, quietly donates to local children's charities, honoring John and building good will.

We decided around Christmas that we'd take the trip, though we wouldn't be leaving until late August to attend the annual Beatles Week, which draws thousands. Who knew where we'd be living in August?

As cheap as I am, I couldn't argue against one splurge. We'd only taken one real vacation in the past decade after pouring most of our money into renovating the humble, but well-located row house whose sale had reaped us a bounty – and left us semi-homeless. Ella's interest in the Beatles had only grown. She still wanted to see George's "castle." We didn't have a Crackerbox Palace of our own at the moment. So we'd have to go overseas in search of a sense of home.

We settled on taking the whimsically named "Magical History Tour," whose pamphlets I had picked up for years at The Fest for Beatles Fans conventions, thinking I'd never take the trip. Now I punched in the tour company's URL almost daily, poring over pictures, reports from past trips and testimonials ("We have always been a close-knit family but this trip really 'bonded' us even closer!" wrote a mom who took the tour with her two sons).

Our journey would be 12 days – more time than I'd ever been out of Brooklyn, forget about the country. I'd certainly never been away from work that long. That made me a little nervous. The other thing that got me worrying is that we were only spending five days in London, and the rest in Liverpool. We hadn't spent enough time there on our honeymoon, but what the hell would we do for a week? Would this turn into a colossal – and expensive – disappointment?

Still, the itinerary seemed packed – visits to the spots you'd expect (their various homes, Abbey Road, etc.) and others even I had never heard of (The Barnston Women's Institute?).

Though the karma was far from instant, we finally bought our humble dream house in February, nearly four months after our blind leap. Now all we'd have to do is rebuild the place – more to the point, hire somebody to do it (I can't hammer a nail without crushing a finger, which makes typing or playing the guitar, the only two things I'm remotely good at, particularly difficult).

I'd get off the subway most nights around midnight, and stop by our house-in-transition. Groping my way through the darkness, I'd latch onto the makeshift light switch dangling from a web of exposed wires and tiptoe through the construction site, dodging hunks of concrete, wood and tool boxes, while trying not inhale the plaster dust from ancient walls ripped asunder. I searched each night for the latest modicum of progress – wow, they ripped out the old sink! – before returning to the sublet and retreating to the chilly back room where I'd peruse the Magical History Tour website.

One night, I walked by our house and was too tired to do my usual dance in the dark. Thank God: When I stopped by the next morning, I discovered that the first floor had been torn away, meaning I narrowly avoided a midnight-express trip to the rubble-strewn basement.

By mid-July, only two rooms – our respective bedrooms – and a bathroom were done. But we had to leave the sublet, and not just to keep our sanity. We were running out of money, and the renovation, of course, was taking more time and cash than we had anticipated. So we moved into the top floor of our new home. Amid the hammering and occasional jackhammering that woke me up daily, our trip to London and Liverpool wasn't just going to be a nice time, it would be our temporary salvation – and an addition to our growing long-term debt.

Our contractor Stanley drove us to Kennedy Airport, on Saturday, Aug. 20, 2005, assuring us everything would be much better when we got back. "No worries," he said.

But I'm a worrier and I was particularly concerned about spending too much in Liverpool. "No souvenirs!" I decreed, eliciting eye rolls from Theresa and Ella. "No lunches in Liverpool! Stock up during breakfast" – a full English breakfast was part of the Liverpool leg of the package.

I knew they would buy souvenirs – and eat – in that order, as they pleased. I just felt obliged to do or say something before our lives spiraled further out of control.

As we entered the British Airways terminal at JFK, each of us lugged a large, overstuffed suitcase. We tend to overpack. But in some respects, our lives were in those bags. We'd pretty much been living out of boxes and suitcases for nine months. I also carried my acoustic guitar, in its hard black case – there hadn't been much opportunity to play music lately.

So I was damn nervous: scared of flying, tight on money, living in a construction site, worried as always about work and praying that this vacation could somehow live up to the huge expectations of our emotional (and financial) investment. Most importantly, I didn't want Ella to be disappointed.

We arrived in plenty of time (Theresa and I share a mortal fear of missing planes and trains), and zipped through security, shoe removal and all, on the sleepy summer afternoon.

We must have been quite a sight as we trudged toward our gate. Theresa, in her black, oversized "Hey Jude" album T-shirt, walking with the swagger that she'd gained as a local businesswoman and from bossing around a house full of construction workers. Me, a year from 40 with the job I always wanted and a walking ball of anxiety who refused to wear a Beatles T-shirt, lest I draw attention to myself (I no longer took my Mets cap abroad – post 9/11, I was worried about sticking out as an American, never mind a New Yorker). And Ella, who wore a pink Beatles T-shirt, a blue skirt and glasses with vintage 1950s cat-eye-style frames.

The movie was a year from release, but she already was a ringer for the oddball title character of "Little Miss Sunshine." After the film hit theaters, we occasionally got stopped in the street by strangers who felt obliged to mention that Ella looked like Little Miss Sunshine, or even to ask if that was her in the flick.

The past year, in addition to our home dramas, had been very eventful for Ella, who was a couple of weeks from starting third grade. She made the beginners division of the Brooklyn Youth Chorus, whose top group of teenagers performed around the world and even had won a Grammy. She read constantly, and finally had caught the Harry Potter bug.

As we walked into the waiting area, Ella carried one of the Potter books and the Elmo doll that had been her near-constant companion since we moved. Only Ella's Elmo sported a tie-dye T-shirt and wire-framed granny glasses she cannibalized from her near-sighted American Girl doll, Molly (we dubbed him "Elmo Lennon").

She did great in school and had friends, though she'd become almost shy after Beatle-related teasing got worse – or at least more noticeable to her – amid grammar school chatter about her sixth birthday party. Ella seemed to get along with adults better than children at times, which certainly made a trip like this even conceivable, but worried us a tad. Were we helping make her an even easier target for bullies?

There were no Blue Meanies to be found on this trip. As we made our way to our gate, we spotted others like us – I was just about the only person in our crew without some kind of Beatles regalia.

We met out tour guide, Charles Rosenay!!!, still the only person we know with exclamation points in his name (I've often wondered how Victor Borge would have pronounced it). We quickly found that his personality lived up to his punctuation.

"You are about," he said with a smile as he handed us our "backstage passes" and plastic bags stuffed with various Beatles buttons and promotional materials, "to embark on the adventure of your lives!"

Chapter 9: London Town

We milled awkwardly around the modest, narrow lobby of the Thistle Kensington Gardens hotel, like kids just off the camp bus, too saddled by exhaustion and initial shyness to say much of anything. The 50 or so of us had arrived a couple hours earlier at Heathrow Airport, via planes that originated in New York and Chicago, though we represented at least a dozen states and Canada. Golden slumbers still clouded our eyes after the overnight flight and brief bus tour around London that basically killed time until check-in.

Ella, though, soaked it all in – pointing excitedly at Big Ben, which, by now, was more than just scenery from "Mary Poppins" to her. Still, Ella wasn't all that grown up yet that she wasn't keen on seeing the stage musical version of the umbrella-propelled nanny's adventures, then a London hit – and an expensive, hard ticket to get, even in a city where theater is a relative bargain, at least compared to New York.

The lobby silence broke with an unexpected – and free – theatrical moment, courtesy of a bald, goateed man of about 50, holding himself up with metal braces. He lifted one brace up and swung it in a semicircle as he asked in a booming voice, "Anybody here like Shakespeare?"

Everyone looked around and some wondered aloud if we were on the right tour, before laughing. The welcome icebreaker came on a sunny August day during what was turning out to be an unusually hot London summer. We became fast friends with Ed, who turned out to live a couple subway stops from us and heretofore would be known to us as Brooklyn Ed. He was not be confused with Ukulele Ed, who was from San Francisco by way of Hawaii and carried a ukulele with him for much of the tour.

There were Pete and Audrey, a young couple and huge Beatles fans from Hawaii who won their trip through a radio contest. There were tour veterans like Nanci from St. Louis and Jilly from upstate New York. They were repeat roommates. So were Dave, a middle-aged Midwestern Rolling Stones fan who loves the Beatles almost as much, and "Sixties" Jim of Queens. He certainly was in his 60s, but got his nickname from his ever-present denim jacket festooned with British Invasion-band buttons (and perhaps also for the glassy look in his eye suggesting he was enjoying one never-ending flashback). There were a handful of couples younger than Theresa and I, and some college-student types, but Ella was by far the most junior member of the group.

Brooklyn Ed loved both the Beatles and Shakespeare. A veteran of the Magical History Tour, he promised to pipe in with appropriate digressions on the Bard as we traveled through London. Charles interrupted Ed's soliloquy with the welcome news that we'd be able to check in early, and began handing out room keys. I'd been on enough overseas trips by now to know that the smart thing to do was catch a few hours sleep, especially with a child who was too excited to snooze much on the plane.

The group gathered back in the lobby in the early evening and headed to Sticky Fingers, a nearby restaurant owned by the Stones' Bill Wyman that was decorated with 1960s rock-star photos, posters and guitars. The joint offered a close-enough attempt at a Tex-Mex menu that sated some very tired and hungry Americans. We wandered back to the hotel, with Theresa and Brooklyn Ed trailing. No Beatles yet, I thought, as Ella and I walked along Bayswater Road, where the appropriately numbered No. 9 bus whizzed by us. But unlike nearly 15 years earlier in Liverpool, I wasn't worried. We were among Beatle people – and we were just rolling up.

I had never met Richard Porter, but certainly knew of him. His reputation as the best London Beatles tour guide, and all-around Fab Four authority preceded him. He literally wrote the book on the Beatles guide to London and gave two-hour walking tours most days. I was still a little miffed that during our last London adventure six years earlier we were saddled with a substitute. He turned out to be excellent, but he wasn't the legendary Richard Porter. We learned we'd be treated to several doses of Porter. Yes, we'd get his standard two-hour walking tour, but first we'd pile on a bus and go on a day-long expedition to obscure Beatle-related sites in the city – the kind of stuff hardcore fans dreamed about or didn't dream existed.

Brooklyn Ed had spoken of the Bard. But Richard possesses a Shakespearean actor's manner of speaking, filled with dramatic pauses and careful diction to imbue even the most banal of phrases – "Does anybody need to make a rest stop before we leave?" – with drama and the air of historic significance. He also has a showman's knack for building up to a moment and springing the import with a vivid theatricality. At one point, he roused us off the bus and onto a seemingly ordinary street in a sleepy, nondescript London suburb, leading us to figure it was time to stretch our legs. He suddenly stopped and pointed at the sidewalk.

"It was on this very spot in 'Help!' that Ringo tried to post a package, only to have his hand pulled into the letterbox by the villains trying to wrest the sacred ring from his finger!" Richard thundered.

Then he opened his ever-present binder of photos to show us a still depicting the scene.

"Where's the mailbox now?" one tour member asked.

"It was a prop," Richard replied, faux-haughtily, as if on cue, having no doubt answered the question many times before.

That was the instant we decided we loved this guy, like only Beatle fans could – he's a master of the delightfully obscure, an eccentric whose devotion to detail and excitement of sharing his discoveries endeared him to a crowd that actually knew what the hell he was talking about.

Our time with Richard yielded many such moments, as he guided us from site to site, some more familiar than others, triggering visual memories and music of the mind at the recognition of things we didn't know we knew.

That Japanese gallery and sweets shop on the corner looks familiar – oh, it was once the second-hand store where Ringo bought his hobo clothes in "A Hard Day's Night!" That narrow strip along the Thames – the *exact spot* where Ringo's camera tumbled off the rock and into the water moments later! Hmm, where have we seen that long, low-hanging tree branch before – of course! That's where John, Paul and George sat for the "Nowhere Man" single cover!

An afternoon rain fell as we pulled up to the old Hammersmith Odeon, the legendary concert hall where everyone from ABBA to Zappa played, with the Beatles, of course, the most important ingredient in the alphabet soup. Some of our group – including Ella – didn't want to get off the bus. But Richard and tour veterans promised it would be well worth the walk in the rain.

A crowd already had gathered out front. Weezer was set to play that night, and we could hear the rumble of the soundcheck going on inside. It seemed unlikely we would get a peek inside the Art Deco theater, then known as the Carling Apollo. But Richard wasn't interested in getting us out of the rain. He led us around to the rear of the building, making us wait as he negotiated with some burly security guards who seem to know him, and obviously weren't too pleased to see him. He went through several layers of supervisors before finally getting us waved in. "Quickly, quickly," he said. "We only have a few moments."

All this to see the back of a theater? As we

rounded the corner, Ella and I looked up and then looked at each other, turned to Theresa and declared in unison, "The fire escape from 'Hard Day's Night!'" This was the scene where the Beatle bound out of the TV studio that was their prison, trample down the metal stairs and bounce around a field (two fields, actually, both far from the spot where we stood in the shadow of an elevated highway, Richard told us) to "Can't Buy Me Love."

And so it went. There were stops at the expected: Abbey Road (where Ukulele Ed led us in an impromptu sing-along of "Something"), the old Apple headquarters on Saville Row, the scene of the "Let it Be" rooftop concert. The unexpected: the pubs from "A Hard Day's Night" and "Help!" (where some wags whistled Beethoven's Ninth, a key part of the silly plot). The decidedly obscure: Chiswick House, the bucolic home of the aforementioned historic tree branch and the statue-filled site of the rarely seen "Paperback Writer" and "Rain" promotional shorts.

The songs played in our heads as we merrily snapped pictures, including the first of what would be many group shots, in front of the white, Romanesque plaster, stone and marble statues of Chiswick House where John, Paul, George and Ringo helped create what would become the modern music video. We were an odd crew to outside eyes – okay, to just about any eyes. But we were loving our garden party.

Our crew returned to the hotel by early evening to freshen up. We were set to meet in the hotel lobby at 7:30 p.m. for another Porter tour de force: a two-hour rock-and-roll walk (and pub crawl) through London's Chelsea that wasn't a Beatles romp as much as a re-tracing of the Swinging London-era swaggering and staggering of the Stones, Clapton, Jimi Hendrix and Pink Floyd.

As tempting as this was, Theresa and I had to remember that we had an eight-year-old with us, something that was at times easy to forget, even as she clung to her Elmo Lennon doll. Ella showed incredible stamina, but we needed to be sure to slow down, lest there be meltdown to rival Three Mile Island. We were, after all, just a couple years and change removed from the lesson of "Tickle Time."

That concept, part of our family lore, requires some explaining: Shortly before Ella turned six, we embarked on the first of several trips to Colonial Wil-liamsburg (this habit would spur some good-natured mocking – any time I put in for vacation at the News, some wit would pipe up and ask, "Which one is it this time – Beatles or Thomas Jefferson?").

My approach to vacations remained, until then, very much like my method of attack on our honey-moon – get up early, go and see and do everything pos-sible with spending as little money as possible, because this may be your only chance. With a child in the mix – particularly one who, as a baby, wasn't fussing only when on the move – we rarely slowed the pace. Quite the opposite: We upped it, trying to expose her to all we could, hopeful that little sponge between her ears would soak up everything as fast as we could deluge her.

About a day and a half into our first Williamsburg visit, we returned to our motel room with plans to head out to an evening lesson on how to fight a like a Colonial soldier when Ella slammed down her right foot. "I hate this trip!" she declared.

I was crushed – up until now, I thought she was having a grand time. She wouldn't take off her colonial girl bonnet (the full regalia would come later) and proudly escorted her American Girl doll, Molly, in the steps of another American Girl book character, Felicity, based on a child raised in 18th-century Williamsburg.

I couldn't look Ella in the eye, walloped by confusion and guilt. "We're doing too much," she told Theresa. "We need to have more fun. We need more tickle time."

"Tickle time?" Theresa asked as I looked up from the adjoining queen-sized bed, where I had buried my head. "What's tickle time?"

"It's this," Ella said, reaching for her mother's belly and tickling it. "It's just a time for fun and for laughing."

So we had a tickle fight and later braved a brief walk in the snow to swim in the motel's indoor pool, which didn't happen to be actually connected to the motel (but what did I expect for $45 a night?). We slowed the pace for the rest of the trip, lesson presumably learned.

We decided that instead of traipsing around Chelsea, we would just hang out, and finally get some rest to fortify us for our last couple days in London and whatever awaited us in Liverpool. But no sooner had we gotten our second wind did Theresa and Ella decide (conspire?) that there would be another famous Brit on the night's schedule: Mary Poppins.

I know a scam when I see one: Girls feign fatigue. Skip evening event that we've basically paid for. Insert new expense we had agreed (or so cheapskate dad thought) to avoid.

But for once, I was ahead of them. This was the hottest ticket in town, and chances of us getting seats barely an hour-and-a-half before show time seemed slim. So I called their bluff: Sure, I'd try. What harm could come of that?

I figured, if nothing else, I'd get out and clear my head a little. So I took the No. 9 bus (No. 9, No. 9, No. 9) to Picadilly Circus, which, with its bustle under the glare of flashing neon signs, got my adrenaline pumping as if I were home in Times Square. I hadn't been to Picadilly in a few years, but recognition instantly kicked in as I broke from the bus stop crowd, outside the Underground station, and fought my way up Shaftsbury Avenue, which I was pretty sure ran more or less parallel to Old Compton Street, home of the Prince Edward Theatre.

I found my way to the box office, about an hour before curtain time, and breathlessly made more of a speech than a request: "I know you get this question 100 times a day from clueless tourists, but there's not chance on earth that you'd have three tickets to tonight's performance, right?"

The terribly polite clerk replied, "I'm terribly sorry, sir, but there's nothing available at the moment"

– *whew!* "But" – *uh, oh* – "there's a chance there might be some returns, so you might want to pop back in a bit, just in case."

I figured I was off the hook. I could, with a clear conscience, call back Theresa and Ella, and tell them there weren't any tickets when I asked – a Clinton-esque dodge to be sure, but entirely accurate. Which is what I did. What I didn't count on was Ella's cheerful "Okay, thanks for trying, Daddy," followed by a sigh of deep disappointment. Her sigh hung over me like a London fog as I wandered back toward the bus stop on Regent Street.

I fumbled for change for the bus when it hit me: What would be the harm in trying again, if only so I could live with myself? He was only going to tell me, "No," anyway. So I made my way back to the window with the same clerk. "Hey, just checking back on the off chance..."

"You're in luck," he said, filling me with equal parts dread, elation and regret. "We do have three to-gether. Now, they're somewhat limited viewing..."

"What exactly does that mean?" I asked, my inner miser sensing an out.

"They're really quite fine," he said. "There's a moment or two when you don't have a full view of the action, but we've never gotten any complaints."

"How much?" I asked.

Whatever he told me, I did a quick conversion – about $225, total. Cheaper than Broadway, but a budget breaker, nonetheless. I paused, but could sense the urgency in his eyes. Others were in line behind me and the show was about a half hour from curtain.

Should I go back to the hotel and say nothing? Should I say I tried again but decided against paying good money for obstructed view seats? Or should I just take out the credit card, take a deep breath and hope for a dispersing of the sigh-of-guilt cloud?

I signed the credit card slip as fast as I could, grabbed the tickets and ran for the nearest payphone. I fumbled for change – I will never understand how London payphones work – and spent about $5 in three attempts to get through to our room. Theresa picked up this time. "You've got to get here now!" I said.

"Why?"

"I got tickets."

"To what?"

"To Poppins, what the hell do you think? It starts in 25 minutes."

"How?"

"It's not important how. Just get here."

"How?"

"Is this 20 questions? Take a cab."

"You're telling us to take a cab?" Theresa replied with astonishment.

"If you don't get here immediately, the $225 I just spent on tickets will disappear. So yes, unless you have flying umbrellas, take a cab."

"Okay, but we're starving."

"I'll get us food. You get your asses here. We're going to see 'Mary Poppins' if it kills us."

It probably would, I thought, as I ran in search of food. I sprinted around the corner to the Pizza Hut I knew was there. I'm half-Italian and from Brooklyn, so I know from good pizza and Pizza Hut doesn't meet my standards. But I always got a perverse kick out of this particular branch. It's located more or less at 84 Charing Cross Road, the location of the fictional bookstore that gives the wonderful book, play and movie its title.

But Pizza Hut was packed, filled with more Brits than tourists. Panting by now, probably more from the impending anxiety attack than my serpentine sprint through the crowd, I made my way toward Leicester Square, and found a chippie selling something called pizza. If nothing else, you could hold it in your hands and eat it quickly. I bought three hunks and a bottle of water, and dashed back to the theater where I found Theresa and Ella getting out of a cab. We joined the ticket holders line and choked down our dinner only slightly faster than the queue moved.

As we found our seats, I told Theresa and Ella the story of how I got the tickets. I warned them about the limited sight lines, though we seemed to have a full view. It wasn't until when Mary takes her big flight through the theater that we eventually were left with a view of only her granny boots. It didn't much matter. The show was bearable and Ella was thrilled. Perhaps the most precious of the hundreds of pictures we snapped during the trip is one of a beaming Ella with the "Poppins" marquee in the background after the show. That alone was worth $225 – or a lot more.

It was about 10:30 p.m. by the time I took that picture, and we due back in the lobby at 9 a.m. for the next morning's adventure. We took the tube back to the hotel (I wasn't going to splurge for a cab after all that, not that we could have easily hailed one as the chattering West End theater crowd spilled out into the streets). As we walked into the lobby, we were greeted by the jangling of guitars and voices that were buoyant if not exactly sweet or in unison.

Much of our tour group had gathered in the bar off the lobby, downing pints and singing "Please Please Me," accompanied by Ukulele Ed and three or four others strumming away on acoustic guitars. It was past 11 p.m., but there was no question we'd be joining them as our third wind of the day blew in. As Ella and Theresa settled in with the crowd, I ran up to our room and grabbed my guitar, which I had brought along somewhat sheepishly, not knowing whether there would be any opportunity to play.

As a teen, I taught myself every Beatles song on guitar, and many on piano, not that this was a talent that came in particularly handy – save for a night like this. Ella could sing like her mother, and knew all the words. She recently had started piano lessons and already could plunk out some simple tunes. I hoped she'd get serious about music and stick with lessons, unlike me, for whom written music might as well be Aramaic.

We jammed, going from rockers ("Back in the U.S.S.R") to ballads ("If I Fell") as the night technically turned to morning. Ella eventually dozed off, her head nestled in her mother's lap.

We played well past last call, but the two bartenders, both apparently German, kept pulling the pints as they shouted requests: "Please, please, American friends! Please do 'While My Guitar Gently Weeps!'"

That was the night our tour bonded as a group, with familiarity turning to friendship. I've since read that singing together engenders strong feelings of unity. Apparently, a chemical sent through the brain during sing-alongs is the same one released during sex (paging Dr. Freud!). In any event, after Charles declared it the best jam in Magical History Tour history, we all returned to our rooms – separately as far as I could tell, though there did seem to be a couple romances blossoming amid all the Beatles and beer. We were happily exhausted, ready for our next adventure, all together now.

The burly biker dude leading us down the narrow, spiral stairs, his hair flowing Hagrid-like from under his bandana, certainly didn't look anything like my grandmother – but he sure sounded like her. Jimmi Ward escorted us into the underground former Royal Family vault, part of the old Coutts Bank, off Old Park Lane. There weren't any gold bars or diamonds to be found, but there were treasures perhaps more priceless to the likes of our crew.

Still groggy from our marathon sing-along, we stood shoulder to shoulder in the cramped, somewhat musty confines of The Vault, as it's known, below the original Hard Rock Café. Jimmi, who speaks with a thick Scottish brogue growling with Glasgow, the seaport city where my paternal grandparents were born, is the vault master, responsible for safeguarding treasures that included John's "Instant Karma"-era Army jacket, Bob Dylan's fedora and guitars once played by Jimi Hendrix, Pete Townsend and other rock greats.

Jimmi told us the story of the first Hard Rock, which opened in 1971 as a musician's hangout. But the memorabilia collection the chain is best known for didn't get its first piece until 1979 when Eric Clapton handed over a guitar, as legend has it, to settle his bar bill. Jimmi picked up the red-and-white Stratocaster in question, waving it with one hand, as the tour members closest to him ducked with each gesticulation. "At the Hard Rock, we don't believe in keeping things away locked away behind glass, like in some museum. It's for people to touch. Now who wants go give it a go?"

Stunned silence greeted the question as it hit us all at once that he was offering a chance to hold the guitar played by the man who had inspired "Clapton is God" graffiti around London in the late 1960s. Clapton, of course, also was responsible in a sense for our new house, which held our hopes and all our money – something I nearly had forgotten about during our trip.

"Play it, Daddy," Ella said as Theresa pushed me toward Jimmi.

I took the guitar, sat and played a few licks of "Layla" before passing along the treasure to the next eager set of hands. I fantasized for a moment about running off with the ax. My daydream, though, focused more on selling the Strat and paying off our bills, than on starting a new life as a bluesman, suddenly infused with some kind of "Crossroads"-like magical playing power coursing through the strings previously bent by God.

Charles promised there would be surprises everyday, and he had kept his word. Nothing could top playing Clapton's Strat, I thought the next morning as we boarded the bus to Liverpool.

Dave, the Rolling Stones fan, brought out the bootlegs, including a rare recording of Keith Richards singing, "Please Please Me," slowly and Roy Orbison-like, just as John originally intended before George Martin sped up the tune into the Beatles' first No 1 hit. Charles somehow got a preview copy of Paul's upcoming single, "Fine Line," and polled us, Dick Clark-like, on our reactions (most agreed it had a good beat, though we couldn't have known then that the bouncy tune would herald one of Paul's best, most haunting albums, "Chaos and Creation in the Backyard"). As we passed through Stratford-on-Avon, Brooklyn Ed, who had asked us about Shakespeare early on, stood up behind the driver, holding the microphone in one hand, and balancing himself on one of his braces as he started reciting selections from "Macbeth."

Ed, we were learning, was a character unto himself. He had been a child actor, a playwright, a comic book and music company creative director who had worked with the Pythons, met George and once parked Paul's car while working as a valet in Hollywood. He was a mainstay on these trips, and word had it that he was a major memorabilia buyer. We also discovered he was involved in a serious accident some years ago, followed by a near-catastrophic illness from which he was still rebounding. He moved slowly but remained fiercely independent, and was a ferociously good storyteller, even if he sometimes tuckered out mid-tale. He had taken to Theresa, who would walk with him even as the rest of us would charge ahead to places he'd already seen many times, but was drawn to year after year.

We were less excited about Stratford-on-Avon than Henley-on-Thames, where we hoped to get a glimpse of Friar Park, George's estate. Charles warned us the stop might be very brief – as in stay-on-the-bus brief. The town, about 40 miles outside of London, was not only protective of its privacy but of Olivia Harrison's, particularly considering George was nearly murdered in his own home by an intruder barely two years before his death. Security officers, in addition to the local police, kept a close watch. Charles told us how on one past trip, George's older brother Peter had turned a hose onto the tour group (they certainly didn't mind – the dousing gave them a great story to tell).

As Charles relayed the hose episode, I could feel water dripping onto my own arm. Theresa was gently weeping. I guess it could have been couple of things: It was Aug. 25, our 15th anniversary, and the realization of having spent that much time with me was enough to drive anyone to tears. More likely (at least I like to believe), the waterworks were spurred by culmination of what brought us on this trip: Ella's curiosity about George's home, and the still relatively fresh loss of someone we didn't know, but admired from afar. And as I learned on that night in the Olde Queens Tavern all those years ago, George is Theresa's favorite Beatle.

There's something about George that appeals to a certain type of fan, and perhaps he ages best in our collective memory. He might be the most relatable. He wasn't a force of nature like John or Paul. But through sheer will and work he turned himself into a great musician and songwriter, and never lost his independent streak amid a world that, as he put it, "went crazy."

I didn't quite know what to say to Theresa as sun and shadow alternately played against her tear-splashed cheeks as the bus wound through the increasingly narrow, twisting road to the one place where George seemed to know some peace, and himself.

As we pulled up, I didn't see anybody behind the wrought iron gates, though the entrance proved momentarily disorienting: The gatehouse is a mini-replica of the sprawling castle-like building inside. Charles suddenly turned into a commander out of an old war movie: "Come on, let's go, people. Move! Move! Move!," he said, tapping our backs as we exited the bus like paratroopers taking a blind leap.

We needn't have worried. We seemed to have the place to ourselves, as we quietly snapped pictures and peered between the slatted iron gates, into the labyrinthine, shrubbery-and-tree-flanked path that, I presumed, led to George's home. During our travels through the Beatles' London, a soundtrack played in my mind – "A Hard Day's Night" as we ran alongside the Marylebone train station, recreating the movie's chaotic opening scene; "This Boy" as we followed

Ringo's movie walkabout along the Thames; "Rain" as we bounced through the greenhouse at Chiswick House.

Now, as the three of us posed in front of Friar Park while one of our tour mates snapped a picture, the song running through my head was the one Ella and I wrote based on photos and emotions, about a place we'd never seen, but had somehow felt.

As I peeked one last time through the gates, past the reddish-brick guardhouse and into the lush, leafy green that stretched as far as I could see, I knew we had gotten it right – we didn't have to change a word or a note.

Chapter 10: Have Mersey

The bus exhaled to a stop by late afternoon as the bright sun began its slow descent. But we weren't quite in Liverpool. Charles had another surprise for us. We'd be arriving in style – at least what passes for style for rumpled, travel-weary Beatlemaniacs, light-headed from diesel fumes and from one sing-along too many. He herded us off the bus, which took off – with our luggage – and led us to a dock.

"We're going to take a ferry cross the Mersey," Charles announced, turning grumbles to, if not cheers, then nods of approval.

So as we came tantalizingly close to the land of the Beatles, a Gerry and the Pacemakers song would be our soundtrack. But hey, we were on the River Mersey, the same waterway plied by sailors who brought re-cords to Liverpool from America in the 1950s. The beats of Elvis, Chuck Berry, Little Richard, Buddy Hol-ly filled the working-class city in the shortage-plagued post-World War II years with the raucous sounds of rock and roll. For John, Paul, George and Ringo, the river represented a pathway to the rest of the world – most prominently America, a land seen in the movies and heard in those precious 45s.

For us, on this late August afternoon, the river represented the final leg of our journey to the home of the Mersey Beat. We were pilgrims looking not for our Plymouth Rock, but for, well, rock and roll. "Ferry Cross the Mersey" played repeatedly as we bobbed atop the river. I felt bad for the crewmembers who, no doubt, were ready to strangle Gerry Marsden on sight.

I'm scared of planes, and I'm not crazy about boats, either, even for short runs. But I clambered with Theresa, Ella and much of the rest of our crew up to the deck, tightly gripping the railing, as Liverpool came into bumpy focus. My memories of our honeymoon misadventure 15 years earlier were in black-and-white. But the vista that now stretched before us burst before me in Technicolor, going from the flat, gray Kansas of my mind to the Oz unfolding in front of my eyes.

The buildings, at least the ones I recognized, seemed to shine. Scaffolding cloaked many structures, some in mid-construction, others undergoing a long overdue polish. Much had changed since out last trip, I thought, as we pulled into the ferry terminal, a short walk from the Beatles Story museum.

The bus met us not far from the dock. We wound our way through what were once again familiar streets, past Lime Street Station to the Adelphi Hotel in the heart of the City Centre. The stone hotel stands perched on a hill, overlooking a mix of 19th-century buildings and more modern malls, with Mathew Street tucked away in the mix. We shuffled with our suitcases through the extra-wide revolving doors into the lobby.

I didn't know much about the Adelphi (pronounced Adel-fee) other than that it was once considered Liverpool's grandest spot and that the Beatles stayed there on their final return home as a group at the height of Beatlemania (Roy Rogers – and Trigger – also were famous guests). Directly across the street stood Lewis's, a department store where Paul briefly worked. The Beatles and legions of other Liverpudlians used to meet in front of the store, under a door-top statue of a naked man cheekily nicknamed "Dickie Lewis" (as in "See you at Dickie's").

The Adelphi opened in 1912 to coincide with the launch of the Titanic, which was registered in Liverpool, the hometown of some of the ill-fated vessel's crew. The lobby looked like it hadn't changed much since then – for better and worse. We stood in the midst of shabby English grandeur. The gem hadn't been dusted in a while, but in the right light (and with enough Guinness) glimmered with past glories.

The well-worn carpeting was all but obscured by scores of new arrivals lugging seemingly as many guitars as suitcases. Long hair flowed, even on men old enough to be bald. The scene wasn't all that different from some of the fan conventions we'd attended. Only here a melodic mélange of languages filled the room, competing with the "Please Please Me" album playing over the public address system. English mixed with flowing Spanish, Portuguese, Italian, French amid staccato bursts of German and Japanese.

As Charles headed to the busy reception desk, our group stood in a corner near the booth for Cavern City Tours, the outfit that essentially created International Beatles Week about a decade before. Theresa and Ella already were checking out the T-shirts as Charles returned with wristbands guaranteed to get us in to every Beatles-related event in town, including access to the Cavern Club.

The hotel's ballroom and its various bars would be transformed into nightclubs for the week, with the music scheduled to go until the 1 a.m. last call, but – nod, nod, wink, wink – really until 4 a.m. or later. We got our room keys, which, unlike the electronic pass-cards ubiquitous in most hotels, were hunks of worn metal attached to a narrow block of wood, like bath-room keys from an ancient school. Only one key per room – you were supposed to leave the key in a drop box at the front desk when leaving and retrieve it upon return. The system cut down on comings and goings, which wasn't a big deal for us, but could cramp the style of the younger set, especially those with room-mates for the trip.

We took the elevator to the fourth floor, and rolled our suitcases down a series of long, dingy hall-ways reminiscent of the cursed resort in "The Shining." "Where's the little boy shouting 'redrum' and the twin girls on the tricycles?" I asked.

Ella laughed. She clearly didn't get the refer-ence, but was just giddy as we were – not only about our appealingly peculiar surroundings but the promise of fun to come.

Any fears about not having enough to do in Liverpool were allayed by the updated, three-page, single-spaced agenda Charles handed us. Just about every major attraction – and others we'd never heard of – was covered. But to our disappointment, we were shut out of John and Paul's boyhood homes, which had been turned into museums of sorts by England's National Trust since our honeymoon visit. The tours were carefully timed and limited to small groups, and the town was teeming with enough visitors to fill the Albert Hall a few times over. Veterans of past Magical History Tour excursions grumbled that visits to the homes had been included in previous trips. Not that we were complaining.

All we could think about was getting to the Cavern.

From our perch atop the Adelphi, we happy fools on the hill made our way across Renshaw Street, dodging the taxis that navigated torn-up patches of street. Construction was in full swing all over as Liverpool already was preparing for its upcoming year-long stint in 2008 as the European Capital of Culture.

We crossed into the traffic-free shopping center strip Theresa and I had last trodden 15 years earlier. It was packed not only with people, but with new stores.

The three of us turned right onto Mathew Street, which was nearly impassible, especially in front of the Cavern. Sure, it's not the original club – for one thing, the new Cavern is across the street. And the story about the replacement being built primarily with the same bricks as the original needs to be taken with the same grain of salt as any story you'd hear in a Liverpool bar more than a pint into the conversation.

But we were standing in the street where the young Beatles played lunch-hour concerts, slowly building a following that would soon expand to the world. Yeah, the building wasn't exactly the same, but we were standing on the same street Paul where carried Stuart Sutcliffe's old bass, the one Stuart bought for 75 pounds with winnings from an art contest, the one Paul later restrung for a left-hander. Where George wielded his first Rickenbacker and John lugged the amplifiers he "borrowed" from the Liverpool College of Art, about a mile away on Hope Street.

We wouldn't, of course, be seeing the Beatles, only playing a ghostly guessing game of who-stood-where on the street where their music came to life. But we would be seeing a Rutle: Neil Innes, the Beatle and Python pal, the only person to appear in both "Magical Mystery Tour" (with his Bonzo Dog Band) and "Monty Python and the Holy Grail" (as not-so-brave Sir Robin's cheeky minstrel). Innes wrote the Beatlesque songs that filled "All You Need is Cash," Pythoner Eric Idle's irreverent, yet loving tribute to the Fab Four, which became the first rock mockumentary, six years before "This is Spinal Tap" turned up the volume to 11 on the genre.

Innes, who played Ron Nasty, the dour John Lennon stand-in, billed his Cavern gig as the farewell performance of Rutles, though he'd said that before. We'd seen him do a couple Rutles tunes at fan conventions in the past. Heck, I had watched him perform at the storied Bottom Line in Greenwich Village nearly 20 years earlier. I wasn't much older than Ella when the first Rutles music video, a one-off joke at the time, debuted on "Saturday Night Live," a response of sorts to show producer Lorne Michael's offer to give the Beatles $3,000 to reunite (John and Paul were watching

the show together that night and briefly mulled taking
what would have been an historic – and short – cab
ride from the Dakota to 30 Rock).

Ella had worn out our VHS tape of "All You
Need is Cash," and worn out our ears with her laughter,
even if she didn't immediately get all the jokes. It was
like reading a MAD magazine movie satire before seeing the movie. At least she had some familiarity with
Innes, even if she was still adjusting to the shock of
seeing familiar figures emerge decades older than their
captured-on-film prime.

A crowd queued outside as the red neon sign
over the doorway, glaring "The Cavern Club," cast an
eerie glow on the stone pavement of the narrow strip
that really should have been called Mathew Alley. Our
wristbands got us past the line of folks outside and into
the doorway leading to a dimly lit, winding staircase
reminiscent of a subway entrance.

Maybe it was the excitement, the anticipation,
the long trip from London, but on way down the stone
steps, Ella froze – then freaked. "I don't like this place,
there are too many bricks," she said. "I want to go back
to the hotel."

"What are you talking about?" I asked.
"Our house is made of bricks."

"Not like these. Our bricks aren't red."

"The bricks on our old house were red."

"I think I have a fear of bricks."

The dialogue would have struck Beckett as too
absurd for the stage. But nobody was waiting for us
as a growing crowd filed past us, leading to a creep-

ing feeling of claustrophobia. We were headed for a meltdown – and not just Ella. Theresa and I were literally steps away from finally seeing this faux Cavern, 15 years after finding it shuttered on our honeymoon. Now we were arguing with a child who chose this, of all moments, to start acting her age, even if she picked a crazy way of taking a stand against her parents' nonstop insanity. Our failure to bother eating dinner before excitedly embarking on our new Liverpool adventure only added to our collective frazzle.

"I'll get her some food," Theresa said. "You go in first. We'll just have to switch on and off and take turns staying with her outside if she doesn't calm down."

I didn't argue. While bouncing down the stairs, I didn't hear the music, as much as feel it. As dark and as hot as it was – damn, I really should have changed into those shorts, I thought as I pulled out my shirttail to wipe the steam from my glasses – it was less sensory deprivation than sensory overdrive.

The tiny stage stood at the end of what looked like an ancient, narrow vaulted subway tunnel. The band played "Twist and Shout" loud and fast, amid a crush of bodies that seemed to slide off one another, thanks to the humidity. The music roared like an oncoming train. I felt my breast bone vibrate and what little hair I had left fluttered as if I had been transported to the old Maxwell "Ride of the Valkyries" commercial.

This wasn't Neil Innes, but I didn't mind. I was a little confused, though. The set-up appeared straight out of those old black-and-white pictures and that precious rare footage of the Beatles banging out "Some

Other Guy" just as they were starting to hit it big. But my conception of this new edition of the Cavern came from the 1999 Paul special, in which he played old favorites with a band that included David Gilmour, whose Cavern history dated to Pink Floyd. It turned out Paul was playing the big room – an addition to the club, a much larger, open space with less overpowering acoustics, though fine sound. I squeezed my way into the larger backroom just in time for the start of Innes' set.

I found some of our tour mates, including Jeff and Jack, two brothers from Philadelphia, Theresa's honorary hometown, who had joined the trip for the Liverpool leg. They shared a sarcastic, northeastern wit familiar and easy for me to fall into, especially given that most of our other tour companions generally came from the polite majority of the U.S. I ordered a 1664 beer (I'm too much of a lightweight for Guinness), bought some crisps that would substitute for dinner and bellied up to the tall, round pub table. I already was feeling a tad guilty, and missing Theresa and Ella. Our happiest times generally involved sharing music and laughs. This was an opportunity for both.

A few songs into the set, I spotted Theresa dragging in a reluctant Ella, whose face sported the forlorn look of a kid from a Dickens novel being dumped at the orphanage ("Please, sir – can I have some more? Or in this case, less?"). We got her up on a stool just as Innes played the opening chords to one of our favorites, the Lennonesque piano ballad, "Cheese and Onions," a selection, in the Rutles' alternate universe, from the classic animated film, "Yellow Submarine Sandwich."

That was enough – along with all the crisps she could eat – to put Ella at ease and make her forget about the bricks, though a few more songs turned her newly serene look into sleep-eyed exhaustion. It was time to declare victory and leave.

We trudged uphill, giddily tired and all relieved to arrive at our thankfully stone, brick-free hotel, where we finally got a good look at our room – a mini-suite really, with a not-quite-queen-sized bed in one room and a single in a prison cell-like cubby, separated by a bathroom. It wasn't quite 10 p.m., but the hotel rocked with live music blasting from two bars, two restaurants and various ballrooms where bars on wheels were rolled in. Our room faced a courtyard onto which wafted one big jangly Beatlesque chord. "I'm going to bed," Ella announced, and collapsed into sleep within seconds, without taking off her clothes.

"Well, you got the first shift on the Cavern, I get the first shift on the hotel bar," Theresa declared, taking the key on the big wooden block and leaving me in front of the TV with its boring non-cable lineup of gardening shows and cricket recaps.

I arose with a start when she returned a little before 1 a.m., which was when the revelry allegedly was supposed to end. But I shook the sleep from my eyes and headed downstairs, dodging partiers who gleefully stumbled through the hallways, singing.

I wandered into one of the Adelphi's larger bars in time to catch the Prellies – called so after the nickname of the uppers the young Beatles downed to keep them going during all-night gigs playing dives in the notorious Reeperbahn, Hamburg's red-light district. The Prellies' conceit is that they're the Beatles during this period, complete with the eating, drinking and acting up on stage. One of guitarists wore a toilet seat around his neck as John famously had, circa 1960. The crowd played its part, yelling "Mach schau!" ("Make show!") as the German audiences filled with sailors, whores and all-around tough guys shouted during those wild early years.

The Prellies played cover songs the Beatles favored as teens – "Slow Down," "Sweet Little Sixteen" – with a punk manic energy, reminiscent of the Star-Club recordings from Hamburg, a good 15 years before the Sex Pistols. It proved impossible to get a beer, given the throngs at the bar for the never-ending last call. It was even tougher not to move to this music, which was as close as I probably would ever get to this kind of early Beatles experience.

I was distracted, though, by nagging guilt: We'd obviously pushed Ella too far. Theresa, usually the voice of reason, let her own excitement get the best of her. It was kind of cool, though, that she also was caught up with reliving our honeymoon, 15 years later – sans all the sex (a double win for her, no doubt). We were barely halfway through the vacation of our lives. Even if we were behaving like teenagers, we had to remember we were dealing with an eight-year-old who at least occasionally needed to act her age. There was no time for fussing and fighting – we'd have to work it out.

Chapter 11: Sentimental Journey

Theresa and I awoke exhausted and cranky the next morning while Ella was refreshed and raring to go. Even sleepy-eyed, we appreciated the charms of the Adelphi, which included a full English breakfast, complete with slippery stewed tomatoes, which I piled precariously on my plate given my lack of interest in the British ham-like bacon or kippers. I'm not a breakfast person or a morning person, but did my best to be pleasant as Brooklyn Ed joined us, carefully leaning his braces on his side of the table. I didn't have to do much talking – he could go on, regaling us with stories of his celebrity encounters, from Merv Griffin to various Monty Python members.

After breakfast, Theresa walked slowly with Ed as Ella and I dashed to the lobby by 9:15 a.m. as Charles had requested. The early hour brought more arrivals, with additional fans carrying luggage and guitar cases bounding into the lobby, while a handful of partied-out stragglers staggered in from a night that lasted well into morning.

Our crew followed Charles out the revolving door and around the corner where I expected we would be greeted by the imposing, if generic tour bus that had shuttled us from London. Instead, there stood before us the Beatles' Magical Mystery Tour bus, just like the one from the film. Okay, so it wasn't the actual bus – that one had been retired a few years earlier after shuttling visitors around Liverpool for years. But like so much of our trip, this bus, as they used to say in the commercials for the old "Beatlemania" Broadway show, was an incredible simulation. Suddenly, no one was in a hurry to do anything more than snap pictures of the bus, striking various poses along the blue-and-yellow side, bedecked with the trippy multi-colored "Magical Mystery Tour" logo, until Charles hustled us aboard.

As we queued up, I noticed a strangely familiar, pleasantly stout, white-haired lady – kind of a friendlier-looking British Barbara Bush – greeting passengers as they boarded. As advertised, it was Hilary Oxlade, legendary (at least in fan circles) Liverpool tour guide, credited as a pioneer in helping spur the Beatles revival in their hometown. I had read about her, certainly, but I was quite sure I'd never seen her picture. Then why did I feel like I knew her from somewhere?

"That's her!" Theresa said.

"That's who?" Ella asked.

"That's the lady who yelled at Daddy in front of Ringo's house!" she said, sending her and Ella into fits of laughter.

"That can't be her. At least I don't think it is, it couldn't..." I stammered, even as I pulled down the bill of my blue baseball cap and tilted my head toward the floor, lest she somehow recognize me nearly 15 years to the day after I made a fool of myself in the Dingle.

I slumped as low as possible into my unforgiving hard seat when the bus, barely two blocks from the hotel, came to a stop and the doors opened. Great,

Ella with Margaret Grose in Ringo's boyhood home

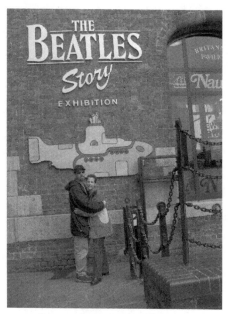

Theresa and Jere at The Beatles Story museum

Ella at Strawberry Field

Crossing Abbey Road

Ella with John's sister, Julia Baird

In front of George's Friar Park estate

Waiting in front of the barber shop in Penny Lane

Ella performing with the School of Rock at Webster Hall

I thought for a fleeting moment – Hilary found me out and was going to toss me onto Lime Street, where not even dirty Maggie May walks anymore. But this wasn't about me: Julia Baird, John's half sister, climbed onto the bus amid stunned silence. She'd been scheduled to join us, even though Charles was careful to manage expectations, always warning there would be last-minute surprises – mostly good ones, to be sure, but not always – on his Magical History Tours.

There was nothing "half" about her. What left just about everyone – even Brooklyn Ed – speechless was how much Julia looked like John: the same nose, chin, the piercingly intelligent eyes. Those eyes were sheepish first at the silent greeting that led to excited murmurs and turned into rousing applause. None of those reactions was particularly fair to Julia, who, while she shared a mother with one of the most revered musicians of his time, proved an engaging a personality in her own right – a woman with a compelling story that belied the toss-away mentions in many of the Beatle biographies.

Even her voice rang similar to John's. She started by somewhat nervously telling us about her family's history, delving into genealogical detail that led into the lives of her namesake mother and the elder Julia's four sisters, only one of which – Mimi, who basically raised John – is familiar to most fans. It seemed an odd way to start, until it became clear that each of these women possessed a strong, unique personality – and had an impact on John, who ultimately would be drawn to the strongest of women.

Sights elicited recollections from Julia in often-unexpected ways. We passed the Oxford Street Maternity Hospital where John was born on Oct 9, 1940, during an air raid. At six years younger than John, Julia certainly had no memories of that day at the hospital, now covered in signs advertising its conversion into condos. But she knew well the family lore of Aunt Mimi running through the bomb-torn streets to herald the good news. Julia also recalled the nearby apartment where Stuart Sutcliffe lived during college – and where John and his first wife, Cynthia, would rendezvous.

Penny Lane might just be a song to most of us, but it's the spot where the major bus lines connecting the Beatles' Liverpool meet (at the shelter in the middle of the roundabout). For Julia, Penny Lane spurred memories of Cynthia working as a clerk in the Woolworth's – the same shop where Paul would buy his combs and send folks for years after becoming famous to purchase new ones because the combs sold there were the only ones that could do his black mop-top justice. We traveled to Stuart Sutcliffe's childhood home, across from bucolic Sefton Park where Alf Lennon met and wooed John's mom.

The landmark-a-minute bus tour and Julia's stories reinforced what we were learning on this trip: Liverpool, in many respects, is a small town, and that the Beatles' world growing up was far more compact than the pictures painted even in the best of the biographies. While John lived primarily with Aunt Mimi from age four, he was still close to his mother, Julia told us – a point she made in great detail in her memoir, "Imagine This," which offers a unique account of John's youth and family history.

John often visited his mother at the home where she lived with Bobby Dykins – Julia and her younger sister Jackie's father – about a 1.5-mile walk from Mendips. Julia remembered John tossing her and Jackie in the air as a game, and taking them to the movies. The home at 1 Blomfield Road was a refuge for John where his mother taught him banjo chords that he transposed to guitar. He and Paul would meet at the house to learn the latest Elvis songs by playing them slowly to catch the words and work out the chords.

Even before Paul entered the picture, Julia recalled chasing a caravan to see John and his first band of Quarrymen play on the back of a flatbed truck. She also watched on July 6, 1957, as the Quarrymen performed at the Woolton fete in the churchyard behind St. Peter's, the day John met Paul.

We piled out at St. Peter's, a late 1880s brick-and-sandstone church, and took turns peering over the short stone wall onto the field where the Quarrymen played, snapping pictures (the grassy expanse itself, unfortunately, was off limits). We trundled back through the small graveyard in front of the church, where one of our crew spotted the headstone memorializing members of the Rigby family, including Eleanor. Paul has said in interviews he came up with the name by combining Eleanor Bron, the British actress who co-starred in "Help!," with Rigby, the name of a UK store. But could Eleanor Rigby have somehow subliminally stuck with him, absorbed on what turned out to be the most momentous day in rock history? (We'll take as a much less momentous coincidence that Eleanor Bron apparently is a distant relative by marriage to the Beatle-and-Clapton-loving folks who sold us our house.)

We walked across the road to the church hall, where Paul met John that day, introduced by their mutual friend Ivan Vaughan. The hall, with its plain wood floors, vaulted ceiling and stained-glass windows is pleasant enough, but not much different than thousands of other church halls in the UK, US or elsewhere. But this is where history was made with a 15-year-old and a 16-year-old coming together over a love of rock and roll.

Dave, a volunteer guide at the church, brought us to the very spot where they met, where Paul impressed John with his version of Eddie Cochran's "Twenty Flight Rock," played with real guitar chords, not the banjo chords, and sung word for word.

"I was standing right there when Ivan introduced them," Dave said, his wizened blue eyes taking on a teenager's glint as he described a scene that probably meant little to him at the time, but would make him a dutiful carrier of his witness to legend.

The goosebumps rose, even on this hot August morning in the air-conditioning-free hall that, judging from the pictures Dave showed us of that day, seemingly hadn't changed much in the last 50 years. The juxtaposition of the ordinariness of the setting and the phenomenon it spawned awed us. These are the meaningful moments wrapped in the mundane – the chance meeting with someone we'd spend the rest of our lives with, the moments that only ring as life-changing in retrospect. There's a sense of hope, especially having a child there, knowing that she'll experience such moments to come – and maybe she's already had encounters with grand significance yet to emerge.

"You could meet friends in high school – or people who you've already met in kindergarten, people who can change your life, whose friendship that can lead to great things we can't even begin to imagine," I told Ella as we bought a replica Woolton fete handbill.

Ella seemed less than impressed. "This church is made of bricks," she said.

We took it as her signal that she was getting tired. We piled back on the bus, assured that lunch was on the way – but not before one more stop.

Charles announced we were going to Kensington, which, to our great amusement, shares a name with our neighborhood in Brooklyn. "See, we're nearly home," Theresa told a weary Ella.

Then my Beatle brain kicked in. The Kensington section of Liverpool was once home to Percy Phillips' recording studio – the spot where, in 1958, the Quarrymen cut their first tracks: Buddy Holly's "That'll Be the Day," and the McCartney-Harrison original, "In Spite of All the Danger." The recordings, for years thought to have been lost, surfaced on the first "Anthology" album in 1995.

Our bus parked on a non-descript side street in a slightly rundown area. As we exited, Charles handed everybody a black T-shirt wrapped in plastic, and encouraged us to put them on. Hilary, with Julia at her side, led us around the corner where a crowd of 200 or so filled the street in front of the simple three-story Victorian row house that loomed large in Beatle history. We arrived just in time for the dedication of a plaque affixed to the front of the modest red brick building, commemorating the recording. A replica of the plaque was emblazoned, in white, on our new T-shirts, which most of our group quickly donned.

Rumors flew through the crowd that Paul would arrive at any moment. But sadly, that wasn't true. However, the two other Quarrymen who played on the tracks that day – pianist John "Duff" Lowe and drummer Colin Hanton – were on hand. We'd only just left the church hall a little while ago, but I was getting that same feeling of the extraordinary growing out of the ordinary: a handful of teenagers pooling together a little less than a pound to make a recording in a make-shift studio on a residential block.

Hanton and Lowe sported huge, time-erasing smiles as they held up framed copies of the plaque and yellow balloons were released to cheers. I'd been in Times Square on New Years Eve, but rarely had witnessed a scene of celebration as charming and joyful, even if the scale was far smaller. Charles had told us we would meet people with some incredible stories to tell about crossing paths with the Beatles, even as they lived relatively normal, humble lives. "This is the one week every year where they get to shine," he said. "Give them the respect they deserve. They are living history."

It was apt advice from Charles, who got us close enough to snap memorable pictures of both men and briefly chat with them. He then ushered us to a private reception at a pub down the block, where Guinness, ham sandwiches (ham sarnies in the local vernacular) and vegetable curry samosas flowed as a band played early Beatle favorites.

We sat with Julia, who told us and our fellow tourists how she hadn't gotten to see much of John after he became famous, save for a handful of visits and concerts (besides, she said, she and her sister Jackie preferred the Rolling Stones to the Beatles). She said she had only sporadic contact with John during his post-Beatles life. In the mid-1970s, she said, they shared a long phone conversation about their mother. He asked her for childhood pictures, which she sent. In 1980, John put out the word to his Liverpool family that he was planning a big trip back home – Liverpool, after all was home – with Yoko and Sean, probably sometime the next year.

Julia, a former teacher, seemed more at ease when the conversation turned to the ordinary, and made small talk with Ella about school. But she couldn't help circling back to John, and stories of their childhood, before their mother was fatally struck by a car after leaving Aunt Mimi's house on a July evening in 1958. You got the idea Julia wished her big brother never had become a star and left Liverpool.

We bid Julia goodbye and got back on our bus. We had a couple more stops to make. We swung by the home on Arnold Grove where George spent his early childhood. While the area wasn't as dank as I remembered it from 15 years earlier – by now there was a BMW repair shop on the corner – it was no Friar Park. Our final stop of the day would be in the Dingle.

We pulled up near The Empress, a bar just up the block from Ringo's home. That's the pub on the cover of his "Sentimental Journey" album, the collection of standards he recorded for his mum, who worked as a barmaid at The Empress. If Theresa became tearful the day before at Friar Park, I surprised myself by struggling with my emotions as we traipsed along narrow Admiral Grove. I never thought I'd be back here, and certainly not with a child of my own. "Try to keep off the neighbor's property this time," Theresa cracked, pulling me out of my daydream.

"Yeah, don't embarrass us," Ella chimed in.

I started to snap pictures best I could without trespassing. Through my viewfinder, I saw Hillary knock gently on the white door with the pink trim. The lace curtains in the only window on the first floor pulled back, followed by the click of a lock and opening of the door just a crack.

"Hello, Margaret!" Hillary said buoyantly, as if greeting an old friend. "I have some visitors here all the way from America. Would it be okay if we popped in for a moment?"

The two women exchanged whispers as the 50 or so of us stood motionless in hushed anticipation. Hillary turned around smiling and beckoned us with an outstretched hand. "Margaret is graciously allowing us to visit her briefly," she said. "But very quickly now, and only a few at a time. There isn't that much room."

The three of us got in and out in a matter of seconds. Ella became claustrophobic, and with good reason. Margaret's pleasant living room is cozy, maybe 8 feet by 10 feet. A comfortable spot to have a tea with a couple of friends, perhaps, but far from a meeting hall. We felt as if we were characters in the stateroom scene from the Marx Brothers' "A Night at the Opera" – just open the door and we'd go tumbling out en masse onto Admiral Grove. I didn't have a chance to snap a picture, but noticed photos of Elvis dotting the wall as well as a collection of dolls scattered about.

We waited outside, the three of us seemingly floating above the cobblestone lane. We had been inside a Beatle's house! I hadn't done anything foolish this time – at least not yet. As the last of our group left, I grabbed Ella's hand, peeked inside and said to Margaret, "Thank you so much for sharing your home with us. I'm wondering if I can just impose on you to take a quick picture with my daughter before we go?"

Margaret saw Ella and Ella saw Margaret and there was an instant connection, despite – or perhaps because of – the six-decade age difference. Margaret, stooped by time and not much taller than Ella, took her by her hand and gently led her around the tiny room, showing her the pictures of The King. "Elvis was my favorite," she said. "I was never a big Beatles fan."

She did, though, devote prime wall space to a picture of her with Ringo that appeared to be from a visit in the early 1980s. She told us she lived on the block most of her life and moved in after Ringo's mother and stepfather reluctantly left. Shooing the throngs of fans who climbed over the backyard wall – there was still an outhouse at that point – had become too much of a bother for Ringo's family. "This was bigger than my house, so I was happy to move in," Margaret said.

Ringo's mother Elsie would take the bus most days from the home her son bought her in a far posher part of town and visit with her friends in the Dingle, Margaret recalled.

By now, the rest of our group was getting a little antsy and maybe just a little annoyed. Margaret gave Ella a small Santa Claus doll and a card with her name and address. "Write me some time, dear," she told Ella. "I'll always write back, maybe not right away, but I'll write back."

A smiling Hillary told Ella, "It looks like you have a new friend!"

This time, I got back on the Magical Mystery Tour bus thrilled and relieved instead of feeling like a jerk. Theresa had been right about things coming in time. In this case, it just took 15 years.

Chapter 12: We're Going Home

As if I needed anymore honeymoon déjà vu, a soccer game gripped the collective raspy throat of Liverpool that night. Thankfully, the match was in Monaco. But that didn't stem the excitement. It was a Friday night, the start of the big end-of-summer holiday weekend, International Beatles Week – and Liverpool was playing CSKA Moscow in the European Super Cup, basically second only to the World Cup on the mania meter. We were pretty knackered, so there wouldn't be too much music tonight – at least not until Ella was safely asleep. We wandered around Mathew Street, and up the main strip, which was getting, um, a little happy, with fans spilling out of jammed pubs showing the game.

The match proved almost a repeat of the contest Graham and I attended 15 years earlier. The opposing team scored first, but Liverpool came back to tie with eight minutes left in regulation time – spurring one overjoyed fan to run out of a pub near the Cavern and punch in the glass side of a telephone kiosk. Moments later, a hapless tourist wandered by to make a call, only to be greeted by another happily inebriated fan who stuck his reddened face in the jagged gap. "I hope you like air conditioning!" he declared.

We took that as a sign return to the hotel, grab a snack and get Ella to bed. As we approached The Adelphi, though, I spied a far more menacing scene on the side street: an out-of-control hooligan repeatedly kicking a fallen man in the stomach. Ella, luckily, hadn't noticed this, so I quickly steered her and Theresa to the chippie joint across the street, where we settled down to a meal of fish and chips and halal chicken. The game blared through the shop's radio as drunken folks wandered in and out, slurring "What's the score?"

Once again, I was in the position of praying for a Liverpool victory, this time so I could get my wife and child safely across the street and into the hotel. Liverpool scored not once but twice in overtime, setting off a happy frenzy, which was only just slightly less disturbing than an angry frenzy.

We dodged the fans and beeping cars to make it into the packed lobby, daring to breathe only after the elevator left us at the long, empty hallway leading to our room. We quickly fell asleep in our happily cozy mini-suite, not much smaller than Ringo's house.

We entered Strawberry Field (no "s" on the real thing), not through the iconic red gates that served as the locked backdrop for thousands of tourist pictures, but through a wider, nondescript delivery entrance about 100 yards up Beconsfield Road. A swirl of music drifted from the bandstand somewhere up the winding path, but the tune dancing in our heads was "Strawberry Fields Forever."

Charles' magical wristbands got us into what was billed as the final garden party at Strawberry Field, the former Salvation Army home for children. John loved to attend fetes there with Aunt Mimi as a boy.

As a confused teenager, he'd seek quiet sanctuary in the place where, at least in song, nothing is real. The sad reality was that the children's home had closed a few months earlier and the rambling property was on the market, its future uncertain. "We don't want them to turn it into a McDonald's," said a local manning one of a line of carnival games, raising money for a Strawberry Field preservation fund, a pound at a time.

The music grew louder as we dropped a few pounds on the games of chance, wending our way up the path, finally reaching the back of the bandstand that faced out onto a sprawling playground. Ella, in her own version of the Beatles fire-escape bolt from "A Hard Day's Night," dashed from our sides and went straight for the slide. While the yard bustled with Beatles fans and locals, there weren't many kids. Ella had the swings, the webbed climbing structure and the self-propelled merry-go-round almost all to herself. The relatively new equipment – probably 1970s or 1980s vintage – certainly post-dated John. But Ella was playing in a spot where he and so many other Liverpudlian youth had whittled away similar days under the blue suburban skies.

Theresa and I got to relax a bit in the sun, watching the various bands, pretty much all of which, not surprisingly, weighed in with a version of "Strawberry Fields Forever." I noticed Brooklyn Ed perched on a hill near the main building of the complex, snapping picture after picture of the happy scene.

We felt a strong connection between the song and the place, not to mention the namesake spot in

Central Park. But watching Ella, who had been reluctant to run and climb since an operation on her knee a couple of years earlier now playing with abandon, a spirit of childhood and hope filled this Strawberry Field.

Ella got to be a kid for the afternoon, as she would again that Monday when the streets of Liverpool turned into one big party. Music poured from a half-dozen music stages scattered through the City Centre, with fair rides and food booths lining much of the rest of the vehicle-free streets. After Ella and I survived our harrowing, if quick, descent down the giant inflatable slide, she moved onto less adventurous frolics, sticking to bouncy tents and the UK version of the Frog Hopper.

But music called all around us. After Ella tired of the rides and corn dogs, we fought our way through the crowd to the main stage, where we were happily pinned in for shows by the McCartney cover group, Banned on the Run, along with tribute acts celebrating The Who, U2 and David Bowie. To my and Theresa's surprise, Ella didn't want to leave, despite the lack of a readily available toilet and my protestations that we risked sunburn.

We edged our way toward the stage with each change in performer, as anticipation grew for the final, headliner act – not a Beatles cover group, but one dedicated to their primary homegrown rival for UK affections: Queen. Dios Salva La Reina – "God Save the Queen" – hails from Argentina, but is loved in Liverpool, where many miss Freddie Mercury as much as Beatles fans miss John and George.

The growing throngs behind us for as far as we could see suggested that all of Liverpool was set on catching the 5 p.m. show. Much more than a love of Queen fueled the crowd's spirits. The only spots on the grass not occupied by revelers were taken up by coolers-full of beer. Some enterprising folks even set up wooden mini bars, stocked with a greater array of booze.

While most of the adults seemed to handle their liquor relatively well, gangs of young yobs-in-training, no older than 14, became increasingly rowdy. By this time, we were smack up against the fence separating the stage from the restless audience. A dozen drunken teens kept surging forward, as Theresa and I surrounded Ella. As I took a deep breath, dug my blue Sketchers sneakers into the beer-slicked grass and steadied myself for the human pinballs bouncing off my already bad back, my mind filled with visions of tabloid headlines: "FLATTENED! Irresponsible Parents and 8-Year-Old Crushed to Death in Rock Riot." While I took a defensive posture, Theresa launched an offensive, during which the young hooligans learned she could out-curse them and then some. "Back off, you little bastards," she growled.

But that only seemed to egg them on. For Ella, her usual calm self during all of this, her only discomfort came when her mother engaged the yobs, eliciting embarrassed rolls of her eyes. "Mom, just be quiet and maybe they'll stop," she pleaded.

Two stage-side security officers, a man and woman in yellow windbreakers, who had been pretending not to notice the impending disaster, finally approached and shouted at the young thugs. This ignited a chant of "Fuck the police!" that quickly rippled through the crowd, like a verbal version of "The Wave." We would have left, if only out of humiliation. There was nowhere to go, however, but over the fence, which we briefly considered.

We soon were rescued by God Save the Queen, which bounded onto the stage with, if memory serves, "I Want to Break Free." During high school, I blew a chance to see Queen at Madison Square Garden during their last U.S. tour. This was as close as I would get. For all the Beatle cover bands we've seen, my favorites are the ones that strive to bring the music to life – sans collarless suits, Sgt. Pepper costumes and faux Liverpudlian-accented patter between songs. There's a thin line between playing homage and cheesy imitation, though I'd never fault musicians for making a living in shows like "Beatlemania."

But I had to admit, in this case, the visuals helped: Singer Pablo Padin embodies Freddie Mercury, not only in voice and looks, but in style. "Radio Gaga," I song I hadn't particularly liked until this point, morphed into the 1985 Live Aid version at Wembley Stadium, as Padin led the crowd in a version that matched Mercury fist pump for first pump. When the group returned for the inevitable encore of "Bohemian Rhapsody," the crowd bounced in time, like the car scene from "Wayne's World" magnified a thousand fold. The rolling mosh pit reminded me how trapped we were, and as Padin sang, "Nothing really matters to me," I started to look around in vain for clues on how we would make our exit.

"Keep your heads down and walk when I tell you to walk – and don't stop until I tell you to," I told Theresa and Ella, in my full melodrama mode.

The crowd, though, quickly dispersed. We were at front of the stage, but at the very end of the line of marchers clanking across of a carpet of crushed beer cans, most of them Carling, the primary sponsor of the Liverpool Football Club. With our ears numb from hours of standing in front of the giant speakers, the crunching echoed like deadened dings of a high-hat cymbal. I turned around to see a sea of crushed cans glimmering in the setting waterfront sun, like a flattened aluminum rainbow leading to the now empty stage.

After another stop at the halal chippie, Theresa settled in for the first hotel shift with a happily exhausted Ella. I went to see the incredible Fab Faux at the Carling Academy, thinking for a moment that they might just be the second-best tribute band on Earth, even if still the greatest group to tackle the Beatles' catalogue.

After I returned, Theresa headed down into the hotel bars for an annual end-of-Beatles-Week revel known as Ringo's Bus Pass Party (nobody seemed to know why they called it that. After all, it was George's father who worked as a bus conductor). I skipped my usual frustrating slog through the UK TV stations and started writing notes in my Daily News reporters pad, cataloguing the scores of pictures we'd taken with our new Canon point-and-shoot digital camera. I expected Theresa to come in by 1 a.m. so I could head downstairs for some fun. But by 1:30, she still wasn't back and, more than slightly annoyed, I fell asleep in my clothes.

Sometime around 4 a.m., Theresa staggered in and crawled into bed. I awoke and we laughed while replaying the ride down the slide and our brush with trampling at the concert. We were in our own little happy world, with no idea that at just about the time of the slide adventure, Hurricane Katrina had made landfall, and as we were protecting Ella from the surging concert crowd, the 17th Street Canal levee broke in New Orleans.

Uninformed murmuring about the growing disaster back home filled the hotel dining room as we downed a quick breakfast and boarded the Magical Mystery Tour bus by 9:15 a.m. for our final Liverpool adventure of the trip. Most of our crew, who had been out in the wee hours, had only heard snippets about New Orleans and Mississippi getting hit unusually hard by a hurricane. I bristled without a newspaper or access to any fresh information, my workplace adrenaline kicking in. But I knew I had to be patient and try to enjoy the remaining hours of our trip.

This was to be our last and longest tour, led again by Hillary. Charles billed it as the Liverpool outing that "separates the fans from the fanatics." We headed back across the Mersey to Wirral, a Liverpool suburb familiar to most of us only as a nice part of town where Paul bought his dad a house after hitting it big. We stopped in front of the house, which seemed like a typical handsome, if hardly sprawling, suburban home, notable only for having more protective greenery than nearby abodes (Paul, we were told, still owns the property, which he uses for family parties. He also stays there when he comes to town to work with students at the Liverpool Institute).

Paul likely first passed by the house when the Beatles gigged at nearby Hulme Hall, a 1950s-style wedding and banquet establishment (its website notes that the "fabulous local band" performed there). Once again, we stood in a spot whose ordinariness belied its place in Beatles history: John, Paul and George played their first show with Ringo there in August 1962 after the firing of Pete Best – giving humble Hulme Hall as good a claim as any spot to being the birthplace of the Beatles.

We moved onto the not quite as important, but decidedly more charming hall at the Barnston Women's Institute, which wasn't much bigger or any fancier than the parish house at St. Peter's. We got off the bus and walked up a dirt path, spotting cows off in a field whose rural serenity seemed out of place with the gritty Liverpool to which we'd become accustomed. The Women's Institute is part of what is roughly the UK equivalent of a 4-H club. We were greeted at the door by a group of friendly middle-aged ladies in Ann Taylor-style dresses who immediately started pressing scones and cups of tea into our hands.

We made our way to the stage, where the Beatles played in 1962 in a performance that marked their first show in the iconic collarless suits Brian Epstein made them wear. An old piano stood in front of the stage. It had been there as long as any of the ladies could remember, though none knew whether it was around when the Beatles played or whether Paul ever tickled its ivories. As we munched scones and shared small talk, the normally shy Ella quietly walked over to the piano and started softly tapping on the keys, giving way to chords that banged out "Twist and Shout." Charles and the rest gathered around for what would be our last group sing-along in a hall where the Beatles likely performed the same song.

Our long, satisfying day of travels into Beatle obscurity ended with another ferry across the Mersey in time for dinner. Theresa, Ella and I decided to skip the final Liverpool item on Charles' itinerary – a private party at the Cavern. We were tired, needed to pack, bathe and catch some sleep so we could be in the lobby by 4:30 a.m. to catch our bus to Heathrow Airport.

I wasn't as concerned about getting enough sleep as I was finding out what was happening back home. A BBC News feed on our TV offered haunting images: the packed Superdome. The pleas for help from folks stranded on water-lapped rooftops. Homes and cars submerged. The words coming from newscasters were even more horrifying: reports of hundreds missing. The maddening lack of assistance. The seemingly nonexistent federal response. The BBC coverage focused as much, if not more, on the devastation wrought in Mississippi.

I felt heartbroken, furious and maddeningly useless – at least if I was in my newsroom, I could have the illusion I was doing something to somehow help.

By the time we gathered in the Adelphi's lobby the next morning, people were stunned. Some wept. A father and son from New Orleans who were on the tour already had taken a cab to the relatively close Manchester Airport to get an earlier flight back to the U.S.

We rode the bus to Heathrow largely in silence, not just because of the early hour and a lack of sleep, but because we didn't know what to say. As dawn gave way to the morning sun, Charles tried to keep up spirits, playing Beatles videos and running trivia games and polls. Theresa and I were voted Most Romantic Couple for returning to Liverpool 15 years after our honeymoon. Charles gave away all kinds of Beatles memorabilia, including a Beatles baseball jacket (with the number 4 on back) that I badly coveted. But this group proved too fast with the trivia answers, even for me.

Ella received a special gift from Dave, the Rolling Stones fanatic, who, um, appropriated one of the many large "Liverpool '08" banners festooned around town, heralding the even bigger party to come in three years.

We gladly took the vinyl banner, about six feet by two feet, and carefully folded it into one of our suitcases, already bulging with T-shirts, books and other souvenirs. We'd find a place for the banner in our new home, which, for all my worrying and grumbling, we were now feeling more fortunate than ever to have waiting for us in Brooklyn. The banner would offer a daily remembrance of the greatest vacation of our lives – and a constant reminder of a possible return.

Chapter 13: One Sweet Dream

There's rarely, if ever, anything very exciting to be found in the Associated Press Daybook, a listing of ribbon cuttings, self-serving news conferences by preening politicians, celebrity-studded charity events and advertising stunts that make up just another day in New York.

Foraging through the Daybook, looking for an opportunity to grill one of those political peacocks about a scandal we'd uncovered, finding the occasional "brite" (world's tallest woman meets world's shortest man? We're there!) or potentially heartwarming piece (man donates kidney to co-worker? A no-brainer!) was part of my job as City Editor of the New York Daily News.

The Daybook slog trolled the bottom of my long mental to-do list as I arrived at the paper's W. 33rd Street headquarters sometime after noon on Oct. 2, 2005. It was a Sunday, usually my favorite and hardest workday of the week. We had a small staff and not a lot of stories in the can. But we (usually) woke up to a strong paper, proud of our contributions – unless, of course, we got scooped, which would mean a miserable Monday.

I walked the long hall separating the lobby from the newsroom, through a gauntlet of oversized classic front pages chronicling everything from Neil Armstrong's giant step to Caroline Kennedy's walk down the aisle ("Shhh! I'm Getting Married!" reads the headline over a photo of the Camelot princess, clad in her flowing white gown, an index finger over her lips and her eyes a picture of exasperation). That's the Daily News: going from the profound to the profane in the turn of a page.

Judging from the giddiness that greeted me as I entered the newsroom, I knew my day already had taken a sharp turn into the profane. Reporter Richard Weir and photographer Debbie Egan-Chin had tracked John (Junior) Gotti to a Long Island church, which, in our world, was pretty big news. Junior had just been sprung on bail, but was confined to house arrest – save for certain events, like Sunday Mass. Egan-Chin managed to snap Gotti kneeling in a pew, his hands clasped and his head bowed in apparent prayer, perhaps asking for forgiveness for the multitude of sins alleged by the feds.

That gave us a strong, if early, candidate for the "wood" – or front page, to the rest of the world. The pressure off a bit, I went through the rest of our story lineup, consulted with fellow editors and eventually found a few free minutes to peruse the Monday Daybook to start planning the next day's assignments.

I quickly spotted what, at least for me, would become the most momentous Daybook entry in Associated Press history: Paul was set to sign copies of his new children's book, "High in the Clouds," 2 p.m. the next day at the Rockefeller Center Barnes & Noble. The first 125 fans to show would get his autograph.

This really shouldn't have been news to me:

Charles Rosenay!!!, our tour guide through the Beatles' London and Liverpool just six weeks previous had emailed our group a couple days earlier, tipping us. I checked around a bit, but found no other evidence, other than that the book was being published that day.

I called Theresa. "Guess what? Paul *is* going to be at Barnes & Noble tomorrow."

"I knew that," she said. "You knew that. Charles told us."

"Yeah," I replied. "But it wasn't confirmed until now. It wasn't real to me until now."

Then she spoke those three little words that always bring me crashing down to earth: "You're an idiot."

I checked in with the flack at Barnes & Noble. He told me people already were lining up for wristbands to be given out 6 a.m. Monday – and it was only mid-afternoon Sunday. The book signing was a photo opportunity only, meaning no reporters allowed.

That wasn't going to stop me from assigning someone. I copied the event information onto our Tuesday story schedule and left a note asking that any available reporter be sent with a photographer. I probably didn't have to write those words: Everybody in the newsroom knew that I wanted any kind of Beatle story covered, even if it wasn't necessarily going to make the paper. They also knew I had dibs on editing pieces mentioning any combination of John, Paul, George and Ringo. They generally placated me, albeit with a roll of the eyes.

Greg Wilson, a fellow editor and inveterate buster of chops, would go into the stories before I could get to them and change phrases like "former Beatle Paul McCartney" to "washed up former Wings frontman Paul McCartney," and insert other blasphemies, just to see my bald head turn red, first from anger, then from laughter.

I called Theresa back. We decided I would head over to the bookstore after my shift to scope out the line. I made arrangements to grab a couple hours sleep on the couch of a friend who lived nearby, with plans to return to Barnes & Noble around 5 a.m. to collect a wristband. If absolutely necessary, I'd sleep on the sidewalk outside. The overnight temperatures were expected to be in the sixties, and it might even be fun (at least for a little while).

Any thought of leaving work early – I'd been hoping to sneak out 9:30 p.m. or so – gave way to reality when a story popped on the wire out of upstate Lake George: A sightseeing boat had capsized, and there were multiple deaths. Not much to go on, but it was enough to get us started. We rousted Joe Mahoney, our statehouse reporter in Albany – he was the closest to Lake George – and got folks working the phones in New York. Lake George is a long way from the city, but this clearly was a big – and important – story.

We quickly learned the victims were senior citizens visiting from Detroit, and we began looking for stringers in Michigan. By the time I left after 11 p.m., with the story in very capable hands, the death toll was up to 20. Not quite enough to knock Gotti off the wood – not at The Daily News, anyway – but the tragedy earned a sliver of a headline at the bottom of the front page.

By now, I was teetering on the kind of dizzying exhaustion that comes with looking at too many words in too little time, making split-moment decisions that mean the difference between being a hero or a goat the next day. Heroes earned the occasional nod of appreciation, while goats ended up on the carpet.

Regretting that I agreed to even consider an all-night sidewalk adventure, I stomped my way east on W. 33rd Street. As I reached Seventh Avenue, I turned and stared at the glowing marquee of Madison Square Garden, advertising Paul in concert on Tuesday.

It was just about 24 hours earlier that Ella, Theresa and I left the Garden after watching Paul give the show of our lifetime. Theresa and I had been lucky enough to see him perform three times before, but it was a first for Ella, who was excited but worried she might fall asleep – she was still 8, after all, and usually conked out no later than 10 p.m.

The lights came down at once in the Garden and the big screen showed a video of Paul, with and without the Beatles, building to "A Day in the Life"-like crescendo that ended in more darkness. After a beat, the lights returned in a blinding flash, accompanied by the opening chords – D! A! E! – of "Magical Mystery Tour."

Ella turned to us and said, "Is that really him?"

We assured her it was and tears began tricking from under her oversized glasses.

That was about all I could take. I'm not much of a crier – and definitely not a public crier (I eventually learned from getting my butt kicked enough times as a boy in Brooklyn that weeping delighted bullies and only begat more butt kickings). But I couldn't stem the waterworks. Theresa, her arms around Ella, noticed my body-shaking sobs and asked, "What's wrong?" at which point her nose crinkled and she joined in the puddle the three of us were making on the sticky Garden floor. We grabbed onto one another in an awkward group hug – a clutch, really – with Theresa in the middle.

All I could think of was our trip to London and Liverpool just weeks before and how lucky we were to share that experience, and now this: perhaps the only time we'd ever see Paul together (he was 63 – how many more tours could there be?). No matter what would come our way, we'd always have this, and as silly as it sounds, that would be enough. How many other families could say that? Then I looked around, and saw through the tears staining my glasses similar scenes to ours, other families sharing a moment unforgettable and all too fleeting.

Paul, in better form than I had even seen him, ripped through more than 30 songs in nearly three hours. The highlight was a solo set of about a dozen songs, just him on guitar, like he was standing in Abbey Road Studio Two, playing "Blackbird" and "Eleanor Rigby" for his mates for the first time. Ella managed to stay awake, though she dozed off briefly during "Helter Skelter," of all songs.

The show ended, appropriately enough, with "The End." But we didn't want to leave. We ran into friends – some of the cousins whose house we had bought – and chatted a bit. Before we knew it, we were the only concertgoers left in the cavernous arena. A security guard politely asked us to shove off. But Ella wanted to see the inside one more time. He gamely snuck us back up into the stands and waited patiently as we watched a swarm of roadies tearing apart the Erector Set-like stage, readying the Garden for the next night's Rangers exhibition hockey game. We left, well, high in the clouds.

The fresh memories toughened my resolve as I crossed Seventh Avenue. We *would* see Paul, this time up close and come away with an autograph, and maybe a smile or a kind word. What kind of dad would I be if I didn't at least try?

The bookstore itself, oddly, already held a special place in my heart. Long before becoming a Barnes & Noble, the space at 600 Fifth Avenue was a B. Dalton branch where you could hang out and read unbothered for hours. This was a novelty in the late 1970s and early 1980s, long before bookstores transformed into welcoming sanctuaries filled with Starbucks and comfy chairs.

The biggest attraction of the B. Dalton, besides the books, was the air conditioning. A couple times a week in the summer of 1980 my brother, a few friends and I would roll out of bed at 6:30 a.m. and head for the subway. When the token booth clerk wasn't looking, we'd barrel through the turnstiles two at a time on a 60-cent token and ride the B train to Rockefeller Center.

We'd head straight to the NBC information desk at the fabled 30 Rock and pick up standby tickets for a new, live 90-minute morning show hosted by a young comedian named David Letterman. The NBC pages usually let us in, even if the oldest of our ragged crew was at least two years younger than the minimum audience member age of 16. They had to fill the studio, after all, and the show wasn't exactly a hit.

We thought he was pretty funny, though, and he got to recognize our gang when he'd venture into the audience after the show to tape promos. "You guys, again?" he'd say with a sigh and the smirk that eventually would make him a fortune.

Afterward, we'd wander around Rockefeller Center and often wind up in B. Dalton, finding refuge in the bookshelves, usually in the humor aisle, thumbing through the collections of Doonesbury and Peanuts strips. I'd eventually wander into the music section and leaf through the small library of Beatle books, including sheet music that I tried to memorize.

But there's only so much reading even nerds could do on a summer's day. We'd venture out for lunch – usually a slice of pizza (you could count on it being 60 cents – in New York, the price of a slice of pizza and a token traditionally correlated) or a 50-cent hotdog or pretzel. A vendor on the south side of Bryant Park sold pretzels for a quarter. That inevitably ignited a debate on whether the savings was worth passing through the amalgam of vagrants, drug dealers and other criminals that made the park their open-air office. Still, not a bad day's out for a bunch that never spent a moment in summer camp.

Our trips were a nice break from summers that consisted largely of playing, variously, stickball, softball, stoopball, Wiffle Ball, boxball and hardball, save for maybe a trip to the movies once a week and the occasional Mets game. More importantly, our low-cost jaunts into "The City" were a way of asserting our independence and expanding our world past our block as we readied for high school.

As much as I loved the Brooklyn of my youth, I wanted much more for Ella. I didn't leave the country until my honeymoon at age 24 – her first trip abroad came at 2 ½. My best friends were the guys on my block. She already was starting to make friends from far beyond our little corner of the world.

As a kid, I dreamed someday of meeting the important people I read about in newspapers, magazines and books. I forced myself to put aside, if never fully overcome, my own awkwardness and shyness to become a reporter. I would do my best to always make Ella feel comfortable in whatever company she traveled.

Paul, along with Ringo, of course, was at the top of all three of our fantasy "meet" list. If there was anyway I could, I thought as I spied the marquee of Radio City Music Hall, a beacon in the distance on Sixth Avenue, I was going to make it happen.

I should have known better.

I turned onto 48th Street at Sixth Avenue to find a mini-Hooverville of Beatles fans behind blue, wooden NYPD barricades, variously nestled in sleeping bags, sitting on lawn chairs and standing in semi-circles singing. It was one very long block to Barnes & Noble – two blocks, really, including Rockefeller Plaza.

I started counting people. I hit 125 by the time I reached the plaza – the same spot we rolled Ella in her stroller in the pre-dawn darkness four years earlier to see Ringo's "Today" show concert.

There were a few dozen more at the front of the line. I suppose I should have been charmed by the scene: fans from their 20s to their 50s, enjoying a beautiful balmy night, singing "I Want to Hold Your Hand" under the stars, sharing laughs and food, and swapping stories. Instead, I was crushed. I walked toward the bookstore entrance, hoping to find someone I knew and worm my way into the line, but no luck. Some of the folks, I learned, had started queuing Friday night.

For the second time in two nights the guy who never cried found his eyes welling. I crossed to the south side of 48th Street, and called the friend who had offered me her couch, to report it was a no go. I screwed up my courage and called Theresa around 11:30 p.m. "I failed," I told her before giving a quick rundown.

"Don't worry," said Theresa, who could go from caustic to comforting in a breath. "Let's just take her tomorrow. We'll hang out outside the store. She'll see him and we'll go home happy."

"But it's a school day," I replied. "She'll miss school. What if he goes in a side entrance? Then she'll be crushed that she didn't see him."

"For God's sake," she snapped, caustic making a comeback. "She's in third grade, missing a few hours isn't going to kill her. She saw him last night, what more can we ask for?"

I knew better than to argue, and walked to the train station.

For once, the train came quickly – a municipal miracle late on a Sunday night. But as the train pulled in, the orange F on the front car only reminded me of how I felt at the moment: like a Failure, with a big, capital, orange F.

Theresa and Ella were asleep when I arrived home at about 12:30 a.m., emotionally drained, but fueled by adrenaline and a nagging doubt that kept me pacing. Not that there was much room to pace, at least not safely.

Our new/old house was seven months into a four-month renovation with no end in sight. We returned from our Liverpool trip with three livable rooms (still no kitchen), and new estimates of when the job would end – and what it would cost. I already had to start the paperwork on a new mortgage, amid rising interest rates. We were looking at paying roughly the same monthly bill as before, maybe a little more. That didn't exactly fit with our original plan of bigger house, smaller mortgage.

Charles had told us that "magical things" happen to people who take his Beatle trips. For me, it seemed that the only magic trick was watching our money disappear amid pixie dust storms of construction debris. I spent the summer barbequing in the rubble-strewn backyard. With October here, most of our meals came out of Chinese-food cartons or the microwave. Yummy – microwaved chicken teriyaki again!

The whole mess started to get to me: I was less than a year from 40, looking at more debt than ever. I loved my job, but the long hours were taking a toll. I didn't get to spend enough time with Ella and Theresa, something I didn't realize how much I missed until our trip. The house initially represented freedom and space, but now I felt cornered – only unlike a rat, there would be no lashing out, just my usual response of self-loathing.

I slept late into the morning, snoozing through my usual 8:30 a.m. alarm clock of jackhammering and shouting (mostly in Polish – I was picking up some useful curses).

Theresa finally roused me and said, "Come on, get moving. We're going to have to go get her from school soon."

It took me a moment to shake the sleep from my brain and remember what she was talking about. "You mean we're still going to do this?" I asked.

"Of course, we are," she said. "We are going to see him."

I knew better than to say another word. She had that same determined look as when we bought the house, as when she started her business. Nothing was stopping her, least of all me. I showered and dressed, topping off my outfit with my "Yellow Submarine" tie, a birthday present from Ella that I rarely wore. If I was going to make a fool of myself, I might as well go all the way.

Theresa and I signed Ella out of school at near-by P.S. 230, where we simply told the workers in the principal's office that she had an "appointment." Yeah, an appointment with disappointment, I thought.

We boarded the F train, Ella a little sad about missing school (she's a little strange that way), but excited about our adventure. We tried to temper her enthusiasm, telling her at best maybe we'd get a glimpse of Paul, and at worst she'd have a new book to read on the trip back. She was wearing the T-shirt we bought for her at the concert, with a simple stitched "Paul Mc-Cartney" signature across the chest. I had opposed the purchase – $40 and it didn't even have a picture. But as always, I was outnumbered.

We arrived at Barnes & Noble shortly before 1 p.m., walking past the line whose members had gone from peace, love and song, to tired, cranky and desperate to use the bathroom. My reporter's instincts kicked in as we spied the paparazzi jockeying for position outside the front doors.

As a journalist, you learn to quickly appraise any scene: where the entrances and exits are, obvious or otherwise. What spot will get you closest to the person you need to interview. Where's the nearest pay-phone to call in your story (okay, it had been a while).

Besides being a B. Dalton aisle rat as a kid, I had covered book signings at this Barnes & Noble before, and knew how these events went down. The author would sit a table in the middle of the store, back to the north wall. There was an exit straight across on the south side where the author would be led into the waiting car on 48th Street. The author would enter through the same door and be taken to a back waiting room before the signing.

I had chased (separately) O.J. Simpson trial figures Marcia Clark and Johnnie Cochran out that door (she ignored me, he gave me some nice quotes from his limo after I yelled, "Happy birthday, Johnnie!" When doing research beforehand, I found it was his birthday – it always helps to do your homework).

But homework and experience weren't helping me now. The setup had changed since I last covered a story at the bookshop nine years earlier. The photo op would be in the southwestern corner of the store. The old VIP exit and entrance point was now the door where the 125 fans with wristbands would come in. Most of the rest of the store was a frozen zone. I had no idea where Paul would be entering. Rockefeller Center, after all, is a whole serpentine, underground world unto itself.

I started experiencing the sharp stomach pains that come with the helpless feeling of being in the middle of being beaten on a story and there's nothing you can do about it. Theresa and Ella were on line buying a copy of the book, as I grabbed one of the store's events staff, thrust my business card into her hand and spit out in a breath, "Look, I'm the city editor of the Daily News, and I'm not asking for any special treatment. But I've got my kid with me, and all I want to know is what entrance is he coming in so she can see him."

She said, "You're good where you are," and nodded toward the front entrance's revolving doors. "He's
coming in the front? That's crazy," I said.

"Like I said, you're good where you are," she
replied and headed off into the signing area.

It didn't make sense – that's the last place a
major star would be entering. Still, a crowd was joining the photographers and videographers outside. The
bookstore wasn't letting in any more customers, save
for the bedraggled folks with the wristbands who were
allowed to dump their backpacks and sleeping bags in
a roped off section, before being herded into line to buy
copies of "High in the Clouds" and being shunted back
outside.

By now, Ella and Theresa had returned from
the checkout counter. I explained the situation, and we
decided there was no choice but to stay put. Ella sat
on the floor in front of a bookshelf and began reading
"High in the Clouds," perfectly content even as the din
grew with 2 p.m. drawing near. Looking at Ella, her
face buried in the book, I could see myself in her – a
bespectacled kid sitting in the same bookstore a quarter century earlier, tuning out the world and leaping
into a new one on the pages in front of me.

Theresa, meanwhile, peered toward the back of
the store, over the velvet rope separating us from the
book-signing area. I turned and saw two figures, a man
and a woman who seemed to be staring at us. Theresa
told Ella to move over a couple of feet so she would be
directly in the duo's sightline. I knew what she was
thinking. As the man and woman moved toward us, I

could guess what they were thinking: a bookstore full of people, a line outside of 125 people waiting to get a children's book signed, dozens of photographers and not a child in sight.

Except for one.

The man spoke first. "Hi, we were wondering if your daughter would mind very much taking a picture with Paul," he said in a British accent. "She'd be the first one on line and it wouldn't take much time at all."

Before we could respond, Ella started quivering, presaging the tears that sent her body shuddering. Theresa and I quickly flanked Ella, and put an arm across each shoulder.

The woman jumped in. "Oh, there's nothing to worry about. Paul loves children," she told Ella reassuringly.

Ella couldn't speak amid her heaving sobs, but shook her head "no."

Theresa and I started playing for some time as we tried to calm Ella, explaining to the duo how much Ella loved Paul, how we had just returned from Liverpool and that she was already talking about the book and the character Wirral the Squirrel – named, we were sure, after the posh part of the Mersey area where Paul had bought his father a home – oh, and how long have you worked for Paul, isn't he wonderful? We were babbling, of course, praying that Ella would stop blubbering. We asked the man and woman, who had introduced themselves to us as Stuart and Michelle, to give us a moment alone with Ella.

The crying wasn't as intense, but didn't stop as

we spoke to her. "Ella, you don't have to do this," I said. "But it's an incredible opportunity. I don't want you to leave here regretting not meeting Paul."

"Ella," Theresa echoed. "You don't have to do this. But think of how happy you'll be to say you met Paul! And think of how happy all our friends and family will be for you."

Meanwhile, we were drawing a crowd, including a woman who elbowed her way into our family conference and said, "I can go with you honey. I'll be your mother."

We nudged her out of our family huddle. "Ella, I think you have to make a decision now. All I can tell you is that in life you never regret the things you do, you regret things that you don't do," I said.

That at least stopped the crying. "So what do you think?" Theresa asked, as I could see Stuart and Michelle starting to walk toward the back of the store.

She looked at both of us. The tension was agonizing – almost as much so as trying to maintain the calm smiles etched on our faces. Ella swallowed hard and nodded.

"Yes," she said. "I'll do it."

I got Stuart and Michelle's attention, and we were ushered past the velvet ropes to a back area in the philosophy section. I could hear the rumbling of the gathered press and I peeked beyond the shelves to see a wall of photographers and videographers – at least 50 – as many as I'd seen for any event, save for presidential visits.

I shifted to block Ella's view. She was still a

little shaky, and I didn't want her to freak out at the scene. I began telling her stories of some of famous people I had met or spoken to on the phone. I told her how Al Gore gave me an impromptu interview outside Madison Square Garden when I was a rookie reporter and he was a rookie vice president. I told her how Bill Cosby made me laugh. I told her how Tony Bennett gave me a dollar when I went undercover, on assignment, as a homeless person (a long story for another time).

"Famous people are just like everybody else," I told her.

It was a lie of sorts. Some are, some aren't, in my experience. But I had a good feeling about Paul. We had invested a lot of years as fans and indoctrinated our daughter into what I was hoping, more than ever at this moment, wasn't a myth. Oh God, what if he was a jerk to her?

"You just talk to them like you would a friend."

She was starting to relax a tad. "Wait until Charles finds out!" I said.

We went through a litany of friends and family who we were sure would be thrilled for her. We started pulling out particularly obscure names, just to keep her laughing. I worried, as Michelle escorted us past the wall of press, that Ella would have another breakdown – this time in front of the New York press corp.

But she seemed merely amused by the scene as we settled in an alcove near the door where the fans on line outside would be coming in. As we waited, I suggested she tell Paul she recently visited Liverpool.

The side door opened, and a few city firefighters filed in. Paul visited multiple firehouses in the city after 9/11, and, of course, organized The Concert for New York City at Madison Square Garden. I knew he had to be in the bookstore if The Bravest were getting a private audience.

Michelle stayed close and kept Ella distracted with small talk about school. I was far from calm, but knew there was no turning back now. He had better not break her heart...

Suddenly the press murmur exploded into a roar of clicks and shouts.

"Paul!" "Paul!" "Turn this way!" "Over here!" the photographers pleaded.

I peered around the edge of the alcove to see Paul, in a stripped blue suit jacket and matching slacks, standing against a backdrop of "High in the Clouds" posters, striking various poses with the book, giving the thumbs up. By now, we were swarmed by the whole bookstore promotions staff – young women with headsets, one of whom opened our copy of the book to the signing page. Paul doffed his jacket, wrapped it around the back of his chair and settled in behind the table.

It was show time.

Ella tentatively walked toward Paul, holding the book in one hand, and holding mine with the other. I turned around. Theresa was hovering just beyond the alcove. I couldn't believe she wasn't following us!

The flashes, were, well, blinding. I'd been on the other side of that press scrum many times before, but had never experienced the brunt. Ella's eyes, though, focused only on Paul. He asked her name, and she nervously forced it out. He extended his hand. "Nice to meet you, Ella," he said, and shook her hand – but wouldn't let go.

"Let go! Let go!" he said in mock exasperation, as he exaggeratedly shook her hand.

She started to laugh. The tension dissipated. He pointed to her shirt. "I like your shirt," he said, with a trace of the Liverpool lilt that had all-but disappeared over the years. Okay, so now the shirt was the best $40 we ever spent.

He grabbed a black marker and signed the book, adding a little heart. I figured this would be it – God knows, it would have been enough – but I tried to keep the moment going.

"Why don't you tell Paul where we just went on vacation?" I prodded Ella.

She mumbled, "Liverpool." At which point he stood, wagged his finger at the noisy photographers and said, "Hey, I'm trying to hear the young lady! Quiet down!"

He sat back down, put his right arm around her waist and pulled her close. "Now what were you saying Ella?"

"We went to Wirral," she managed.

"Oh, Wirral the Squirrel," he said in a funny, high-pitched voice, perhaps in the manner he imagined the character would speak.

He extended his hand again, and Ella shook it. "Thank you, Ella," he said.

Then he put out his hand to me.

"Hello, Dad."

"Thank you, Paul," I said, shaking his hand, "for everything."

As Ella and I made our way back to the bookshelves, I looked over to see Theresa going as far out of her way as possible to avoid Paul as she crossed the photographer/celebrity scrimmage line. He stood in mock disbelief, and coughed to draw attention to himself.

"Are you Mum?" he asked.

She shook his hand, placed her left hand over her heart, tears in her eyes and said, "This is truly an honor."

The three of us reconnoitered back behind the bookshelf in the philosophy section, where just maybe we had the best story of all about the meaning of life. We didn't know what to say, we all just laughed. It all had happened so fast – he was taller than I imagined. His eyes were kind, yet with a touch of sadness. His hands were surprisingly huge.

Stuart and Michelle beamed. "Ella, you were great!" Stuart said.

We exchanged contact information and prepared to leave as the fans who had spent the night outside began filing in to meet Paul.

The photographers were packing up. The press. Oh, shit.

I hadn't thought about them seriously until now. This could be a problem. Ella's image would probably wind up in newspapers and on TV news shows around the world. I felt weird about having a picture of my kid in the paper where I worked – it could be viewed as an abuse of my position. Then again, I didn't want her photo in the New York Post, our direct competitor, or elsewhere without having anything in The News. That would be an even greater embarrassment. I wasn't sure that any of the camera folks had her name. Maybe we could just sneak out the side door. But no, that wasn't going to work with the autograph seekers entering at a fast clip.

By now, I figured the media would be waiting in front of the store. How were we going to dodge them? I couldn't make out too many of the faces amid the flashes, but there must have been some folks I knew – and who knew me.

We walked outside, to find most of the photographers gathered. They already had Ella's name. They just wanted to know her age and where she lived. I was approached by the AP photographer, Diane Bondareff, a former colleague from my days at the Downtown Express. There was no escape.

I became very worried when I didn't see a Daily News shooter. How could I return to the office with this story and not even a photo from my own paper? I called the photo desk, and was assured one of our staffers covered the book signing, but had been pulled for another assignment before we made it back onto Fifth Avenue.

My next call was to my immediate supervisor and pal, Metro Editor Dean Chang. I breathlessly told him the story. I knew he thought I was more than a little crazy. But he has a daughter the same age as Ella, and an affinity of sorts for the Beatles. He also well knew that the Beatles, along with the Mets, were the two subjects on which any semblance of rationality escaped me.

I segued into my concerns about the photo, and whether we should run something. He said, "Don't worry. They've all got the picture. We've got the picture – and the story."

So Theresa, Ella and I began walking – floating, really – to my office. I whipped out my reporter's notebook and started scribbling verbal images from our Paul encounter. I asked Theresa and Ella to help me reconstruct the greatest moment of our collective lives: What did he say again? Then what happened? What was he wearing again?

We took the same route, in reverse, from the night before when I made my depressing march from newsroom to bookstore. This time, I felt like anything but a failure. Our mission had been an unlikely success, and we were going to get a chance, at least in a small way, to share our joy with others.

"How do you feel Ella?" Theresa asked as we walked along W. 33rd Street, past Madison Square Garden.

"I feel like I could fly, like I want to dance," she said, jumping like a ballerina and landing in a lump on the sidewalk.

Since undergoing a knee operation a couple years earlier, Ella had been hesitant about running or jumping, and a spill was enough to send her into tears just from fear of reinjuring herself.

But she got up and brushed herself off, missing nary a beat.

We barreled into the newsroom, where Wilson, the champion chop buster, sported the biggest grin of all. "Ella, you're a hero," he said.

Ella made the newsroom rounds, getting high-fives and handshakes, telling the story she'll dine out on for years.

We locked ourselves in Chang's office and got down to the business of writing. We constructed a lead paragraph around the image that most stuck with Ella – Paul grabbing her hand and not letting go – and we were off from there.

This may have been the most fun part of the day – at least for me. Working in my newsroom with my daughter on a story, on deadline, fighting over words. "Take out 'obtain,'" she said. "I wouldn't say 'obtain.'"

"Oh yeah? What word would you use?" I snapped.

She shot me the "you're-an-idiot" look she'd picked up from her mother.

"I'd say, 'get.'"

Okay, so at 8 my daughter already was a walking Strunk and White.

I gave the copy a once over as Ella speed-read the book – she wanted to know how it ended. I hit the "send" button, with the byline of another Hester ready to be typeset in our hometown paper. It just happened to be a hometown paper with the fifth largest circulation in the country and a reach far beyond New York.

I was hoping the layout editors ultimately would squeeze in a few paragraphs in the back of the paper with a picture, if only as a sop to me. But in the afternoon newsmeeting, the bosses slotted the story on Page 2, then one of the few color spots in the paper. Any awkwardness I felt about putting my kid in the paper both grew – we were in it deep – and lessened – everybody seemed to like the piece. Even the most cynical of the bunch recognized that local-kid-meets-idol makes for a good brite.

I left early that night to get home in time for the 10 p.m. news. I started rummaging through the piles of unpacked boxes looking for VHS tapes to record any spots on the late news. With the TV remote in one hand and the VCR remote in the other, I flipped and clicked my way through the shows, catching Ella on three channels.

I awoke by dawn the next morning and ran out to buy a paper. You never know what can happen in New York late at night, long after the lame Daybook events are over. Page 2 is a prime spot for inserting breaking news.

But there it was, with a picture of Ella and Paul and the headline, "Beatle Paul's My Pal." There was her byline: Ella Hester, Special to the News. That filled with me with more pride than the photo. The words danced off the pages:

I always wanted to hold Paul McCartney's hand, and yesterday I did – but he wouldn't let go!
When I shook his hand yesterday at Barnes & No-

ble, where he was signing his new children's book, "High in the Clouds," Paul held on tight – and blamed me. "Let go! Let go!" he teased. I laughed – Paul is my favorite Beatle, and yesterday I learned he is funny and nice.

It was a dream come true.

I didn't expect to ever meet him. My mommy and daddy took me to the store because they learned Paul would be signing books – but only for the first 125 people on line. People started lining up Friday! But my mommy said, "Let's go just to buy the book, and maybe we'd get a look at Paul."

I sat in the store and read the book. There were a lot of people – but I was the only kid.

Two people came up to my parents and asked if I wanted to meet Paul. They were Paul's assistants, Stuart and Michelle.

"Paul loves children," said Michelle.

They took me to the front of the line!

Then Paul came in and there were camera lights flashing. He asked me my name and I was so nervous I could hardly speak!

Then I told him that I knew why he named a character Wirral the Squirrel. Wirral is a part of Liverpool. (I went there when I visited Liverpool this summer!)

He said in a funny voice, "Oh, Wirral the Squirrel!"

He complimented my Paul McCartney T-shirt and said goodbye. I said, "Thank you."

The book is great and has really cool drawings! I would recommended it for kids who are 8 like I am – or even younger or older. Everyone will like it.

It's about a brave squirrel forced from his beautiful home in the Woodland, which is destroyed by tractors. He goes to the city, learns animals there are forced to work in factories and decides to help them.

There are some sad parts, but it has a happy ending.

I liked the book very much.

But the story of how I met Paul McCartney is now my favorite story of all.

The phone starting ringing at about 7 a.m., and didn't stop for about week. "Hello, this is Ringo, when do I get to meet Ella?" our pal Alan Mindel asked in a stab at a Liverpudlian accent that had too much New York in it to fool anyone.

Ella was a celebrity for a day at school. Her teacher, Nancy Robbins, a Beatles fan, posted the story in the classroom, and the principal put it up in the hallways (pulling Ella out of class was quickly forgiven). My friends at work made me high-quality printouts of the page, as well as of the photos.

Between emails and calls, we heard from family and friends we hadn't seen in years – including Julie and Graham, whose Liverpool house Theresa and I honeymooned at all those years ago. My cousin Jim Connolly reported that he once met Duffy Dyer (a Mets backup catcher from the 1970s), but had to admit Ella beat him out for the biggest brush with fame in family history.

The most poignant messages came from some of the folks we met on the London and Liverpool trip.

Nanci Davis from St. Louis asked for permission to put a copy of the story in her Beatles room – next to her favorite shot of Paul.

"Woo-hoo!" Charles wrote. "Ella rocks!"

We quickly realized that this wasn't all about Ella. The story resonated with friends and strangers alike because she served as a surrogate for any girl (or boy) who ever dreamed of meeting a Beatle. That she was a kid precluded any (or much) jealousy, making it easier to live through her vicariously.

It was quite a burden for anyone, especially an 8-year-old. But Ella handled it all like she handled meeting Paul – with aplomb.

Jilly, the nurse from upstate New York who we met on our London-Liverpool trip, put it best in an email to Ella: "No telling how the rest of us would have reacted in front of Paul McCartney, but you represented all Beatle fans with grace, dignity and humor. You go girl!"

Photos of Ella and Paul, thanks to the wire services, were published in newspapers and on Beatle fan websites around the globe (in some parts of the world, the lucky girl was "Emma" Hester – one photographer along the way bollixed the name). "Dream" was the word that kept popping up in the letters, emails and phone calls from friends and family.

But Paul would have the final word.

Our friend Al Pereira, team photographer for the New York Jets and a big Beatles fan (and even bigger Who fan), has been shooting music stars for years. After Paul finished up at the Garden, Al followed the tour to Washington, where he ran into Stuart, whose last name, we had learned by now, is Bell.

"I'm a friend of Ella from Brooklyn," Al from Brooklyn told Stuart from England.

"Oh, Ella!" he said. "Tell Ella Paul loved her story."

Yeah, yeah, yeah!

Chapter 14: The Ballad of Ella and Yoko

Ella, hairbrush in one hand and bottle of hairspray in the other, stood in the dimly lit outer bar of Arlene's Grocery, a moderately seedy Lower East Side music club named for the bodega the space formerly housed. Her hair, drooping past her shoulders, needed a good brushing before she would take the stage in the room next door for an Aerosmith tribute show mounted by the real life School of Rock, founded by a visionary rocker named Paul Green.

Though only 13, Ella was by now a three-year SOR veteran, playing bass (she insisted on lessons after meeting Paul), keyboards and singing her way through a bevy of shows that included tributes to U2, Queen, Led Zeppelin, The Who, and, of course, the Beatles. Instead of primping her own hair, Ella found herself on beautician duty for a handful of boys, about 8 to 10 years old, all with visions of recreating Steven Tyler's perennially blow-dried mane.

Two of the lads, one tow-headed, the other a brunette, wore Beatles T-shirts. As Ella brushed their hair, the boys launched into an animated discussion about the group. Their lively chat turned ugly when they bemoaned their favorite band's break-up four decades earlier, quite possibly before their respective parents were born.

"It's all Yoko's fault," said the blond.

"Yeah," the other agreed, "Yoko's a bitch!"

I started to rise from my perch at the bar to set them straight when Ella turned and glared. I stayed put. She ran the brush through the blond boy's flowing locks and said calmly, "That's not nice. And it's not true."

She shot me another look before turning back to her younger colleagues and adding, "It's a lot more complicated than that."

I flashed back to a chilly fall day about five years earlier, not long after Ella met Paul. Her curiosity about him and the band had only grown since the shared dream day we couldn't stop talking or thinking about. She practiced bass with gusto after we bought her a knockoff version of Paul's classic Hofner model. She also started playing the piano more frequently, thumping out simple versions of Beatles tunes and accompanying herself in a voice as sweet as her mother's – a voice that was getting great training during her weekly practices with the Grammy-winning Brooklyn Youth Chorus.

Ella, who successfully auditioned for the chorus just over a year earlier, had been happy to get lost in the crowd. Lately, though, she was starting to overcome her shyness about performing in smaller settings and was entertaining our urgings to attend the relatively new Willie Mae Rock Camp for Girls that coming summer.

We finally had settled into our house, with the renovation completed just in time for Thanksgiving 2005, nearly a year to the day after we left our old home. Before we moved, Ella took a bus to school. My new routine now included walking Ella the five blocks to P.S. 230 most mornings. I treasured our walks and talks, even if on too many mornings following too many late nights at work I contributed little more than the odd grunt as she bounded from topic to topic. This was one of those mornings.

Instead of her usual monologue, Ella posed a question that's fueled more discussion than "Why did the Dodgers leave Brooklyn?"

"Daddy, why did the Beatles break up?" she asked.

This was beyond my capability to answer, even on a full night's sleep.

"Yoko," I barked with as much conversation-ending gruffness as I could muster.

"Oh," she said, and looked down at the side-walk. "Okay."

I immediately realized I could have done better than two syllables. But by now we were nearing school, and Theresa, the excitable crossing guard, already had unleashed her morning screams of "Let's go! Move! Move!," making further conversation impossible amid the dash for the schoolyard. I walked home and debated whether I should tell the other Theresa what transpired, fearing the yelling would be louder.

"What's with the look?" Theresa asked as I walked through the door.

"I think I said something stupid to Ella. She asked me why the Beatles broke up and I blamed Yoko."

"Are you an idiot?" she asked, though the question clearly was rhetorical. "You have a daughter who's finally starting to come out of her shell, who wants to play rock and roll, and you tell her that a girl is responsible for breaking up her favorite group?"

"Well, Yoko's not exactly a girl..." I tried to interject.

"That's not the point, you idiot. You're telling her that girls don't belong in rock and roll, that they destroy music instead of making it. The biggest problem is that what you said isn't even true."

That did bother me the most. Forget the sexist implications (even if Theresa wouldn't let me forget) and how I may have inadvertently torpedoed my daughter's aspirations with one ill-chosen word. I knew in my heart that my gross oversimplification was a falsehood. Many factors contributed to the split, which, like many Beatle fans, I had spent far too much time overanalyzing. But I revealed myself to my only child as a troglodyte who used a convenient scapegoat to skirt a complicated, perhaps unanswerable question. That was bad parenting – and bad journalism.

Our chat with Ella the next morning probably didn't help clear up things much.

"Ella, remember when you asked me about why the Beatles broke up?" I asked.

"Yeah," she said. "You said it was Yoko's fault."

"Well, I was wrong. It wasn't her fault."

"Whose fault was it?"

"It wasn't anybody's fault."

"It's got to be *somebody's* fault," she replied indignantly.

"Sometimes things just happen. People change. There was a lot happening."

"Like what?"

"Well, they all started doing really crazy drugs..."

"Shut up, you're making things worse," Theresa interrupted. "Look Ella, you saw how many people were at the bookstore for Paul. The Beatles used to have that every day of their lives, only 100 times worse. They had a lot of pressure and got tired of it and got tired of each other. That can happen when you spend too much time together," she said, looking up from Ella and shooting eye-daggers at me.

That seemed to satisfy Ella, at least for the moment. Theresa walked Ella to school that morning. I crawled back to bed for a catnap after another late night at work. A well-rested, clear-thinking dad wouldn't have taken the easy way out in answering a question of such importance – at least in a household like ours. Our own little Yoko-gate marked the latest in a series of incidents that underscored how demands and pressures from the job I loved were starting to wear on me, and, far more importantly, on my family.

Some months earlier, I spent much of a summer workday dealing with a very good, very aggressive reporter who was pushing a story I wasn't yet buying. "Hey, it's me," she said in an early afternoon phone call. "I've got a good one. We've gotta run this tomorrow!"

We repeated the conversation a half-dozen times, with me each time patiently telling her the story needed more firming up. I got another call at a little past 7 p.m., just as I had become officially late for the night news meeting. The editor-in-chief stood over my desk in annoyance, ready to drag me in.

"Hey, it's me," she said.

"I can't do this now," I replied somewhat sharply.

"But you need to listen to..."

"No. Nope. Not happening. I've got to go," I snapped before hanging up.

That night, I arrived home around midnight with Theresa still awake, which was unusual. "What's happening?" I asked.

"What the hell do you care?"

It turned out the 7 p.m. "Hey, it's me" call was from Theresa, phoning from our local emergency room, trying to tell me Ella got slammed in the head with a swing at the playground. Ella escaped with a nasty bump. But I didn't escape Theresa's wrath, or, worse, my own guilt.

I'd reached a low point in a growing list of bad-dad incidents. Bottom line: I didn't spend enough time with my wife and daughter, and wasn't always there mentally, even when physically present. Theresa bristled under not only the pressure of running a business but essentially serving as mother and father. Now she was also shuttling Ella to various music lessons – all while putting her own theater dreams on seemingly permanent hold.

I was nearing 40, happy in my job, but wondering if or when I'd ever get control of my life. Ella's growing interest and ability in music inspired my urge

to get back to songwriting, to that novel I'd been thinking about for years, to simply playing more music. But
who had the time? Meeting Paul, for all of us, stirred
feelings of both inspiration and frustration. New
dreams sprouted and old ones were reawakened – but
both kept smacking into reality.

The Yoko story provided good "Jere-is-an-idiot"
conversation fodder for Theresa during the holiday
season. I was still smarting in early 2006 when I spotted an article on the front of The New York Times' Met-
ropolitan section by my pal Wendell Jamieson, who
worked with me at the Daily News before moving to
The Times. Wendell's story, under the headline, "When
Father Knows Less," detailed how he handled questions
from his very curious then-6-year-old son, Dean.

When Wendell didn't know the answers to
queries like "Why do ships have round windows?" and
"What would hurt more: getting run over by a car or
getting stung by a jellyfish?" he reacted like a good dad
– and a journalist. He contacted experts and got answers in easy-to-grasp terms. (Round windows are a
structural necessity because ships don't have corners.
The jellyfish sting might actually hurt more, at least on
impact.)

I sent him a congratulatory note, and said he
should write a book. Seeing his article also added to
my regret in my mishandling of Ella's Beatles breakup
question. This dad, a man my age, probably even busier
than I, took the time to get his kid real answers. I was
right about at least one thing: Wendell quickly got a
book deal. He fired off an email blast asking friends

for tough questions asked by their children. I sent him Ella's breakup query, adding the story of my woefully inadequate answer. Not long after, the usually calm Wendell called, sounding quite excited.

"You're not going to believe this," he said. "I think we're going to get an answer to Ella's Beatles question."

"From who?" I asked.

"From Yoko! She's working on a reply."

I filled with joy, pride – and dread. Now the world would know I was an idiot. But at least maybe we'd get closer to the truth.

Weeks went by as Wendell worked on the book, understandably not wanting to share the answer from Yoko to keep the surprise fresh. "You're gonna love it," he promised.

Wendell and his family were among the many folks at the semi-surprise 40th birthday party Theresa and Ella threw me that summer (the sign on the back-yard door reading "Don't look out here!" proved a major give-away). Part of the surprise was that Theresa hired Charles Rosenay!!! to dee-jay and invited Brooklyn Ed. She arranged musical tributes – friends and family singing Beatle parody odes to me ("He wrote the news today, oh boy!").

I loved my party, filled with kids who weren't born at the time of my surprise 30th birthday, during which all I could think about was heading out to cover the GOP national convention shortly after and leaving my basically bedridden pregnant wife home alone. As much as I edged toward the inevitable turning-40 crisis, the last year had been great: the new house, the trip to Liverpool, meeting Paul, Ella gaining some confidence and sprouting into a promising musician.

But I got my best birthday present – and biggest surprise – a couple weeks later, online. I occasionally trolled websites advertising journalism jobs to keep tabs on whether the competition was hiring. I'd use listings as an argument to hire more staff – or at least to stem possible cutbacks. I stumbled on to a post advertising a job for a news service director at the new City University of New York Graduate School of Journalism, which was due to open in the fall.

I'd been following the school's development in the press. The idea was to provide affordable state-of-the-art journalism education at a time when the profession was in the midst of profound change.

I'd often thought that I might want to teach someday, but when I was past 60 – certainly not at 40. But the listing intrigued me. The school's leaders were looking for someone to start a website that would distribute work from student reporters covering every neighborhood in the city. I saw a chance to guide young journalists reporting the kinds of local interest stories that I didn't always have an opportunity to get into the paper. I sent a resume and scored an interview.

I soon found myself walking with J-School Dean Steve Shepard through a new newsroom, complete with TV and radio studios, staffed by a faculty of top journalists. I began to get excited about the possibility of working at a journalism start-up at a time when innovation emerged as key to saving the profession.

They liked me, and I got an offer. It marked a substantial pay cut, but as always, I followed my heart. I worked for the Daily News because it was my father's paper. I decided to move to CUNY, in part, because it was my mother's school. In her day, CUNY's Brooklyn College, from which she graduated in the 1950s, was the poor man's Harvard, and helped her become the first woman in her family to earn a college degree.

It wasn't an easy transition after 15 years of feeding off the constant energy of the Daily News' newsroom and working on some of the biggest stories of that time period. But I came to love my new job – my colleagues, students, the work. I also loved finally having a normal schedule with holidays, weekends – and nights – off. I transformed into a roadie dad as Ella's musical exploits grew. Theresa began going out at night, seeing Broadway shows, networking, making noise about getting back into the theater in some kind of to-be-determined big way.

Weekends, though, were family time.

About 10 weeks into my new job, Yoko released a collection of her songs performed by contemporary artists like The Flaming Lips and DJ Spooky. She called the album "Yes, I'm a Witch," a humorous nod to the reputation that unfairly dogged her for more than 40 years. Yoko, we learned, was set to sign the album at the Borders Books outlet next to Madison Square Garden, where she and John played the One to One charity concerts in 1972, and where they were reunited two years later at a Thanksgiving Elton John show following an extended split.

We arrived early that Saturday morning to find a considerable crowd. Ella and Theresa got on line as I fought my way through the growing queue to buy a copy of the CD for Yoko to autograph. Security was tight – no cameras allowed. I wasn't hoping for a picture as much as for a moment to ask Yoko what she'd told Wendell – and introduce her to the child who asked the question. I got back to the long line only to find that if we all wanted to stay we'd have to buy three copies of "Yes, I'm a Witch" – one each.

I couldn't bear to part with any more money, so Theresa ran off to purchase two more, swinging back under the velvet rope just as we got our first glimpse of Yoko from about 30 feet away. She looked tiny behind the table, and didn't grow much as we neared. Fans couldn't get close to her: An intermediary would take the CD, walk it five or so feet to Yoko, who signed her name with a silver marker. There didn't seem to be any opportunity for meaningful interaction.

"Don't try anything," Theresa warned. "This isn't Paul. Magic and lightning don't strike twice. Don't embarrass your daughter – or me."

I wanted to say so much to Yoko. Most of all, I wanted to apologize for my thoughtless answer to Ella.

As we got a couple spots away from the head of the line, it became apparent there would be no way to talk without yelling across the ropes and creating a scene. As we handed our trio of CDs to a security guard, Yoko made eye contact with Ella and gave her long smile. This wasn't a witch. She looked like a grandma – albeit a grandma dressed in black, with fancy sunglasses and an aura of cool.

"Oh," she said, waving to us. "How nice. A family!"

Wendell's great book – *Father Knows Less, or: "Can I Cook My Sister?" One Dad's Quest to Answer His Son's Most Baffling Questions* (Putnam) – came out that September and got a ton of well-deserved publicity. Ella's question, my answer and Yoko's reply turned up in media accounts from the Daily News to USA Today to the "Today" show. Wendell also did several book readings, including one at the Community Bookstore in Brooklyn's Cobble Hill, across the street from the Brooklyn Youth Chorus. He invited Ella and me to participate.

Ella asked her question: "Why did the Beatles break up?"

I gave my one-word answer, shrugging my shoulders and turning red amid peals of laughter from parents and kids alike.

Then Wendell, playing Yoko (sans high-pitched voice), read her answer, which might be as close to the truth as we'll ever get: "Because they all grew up, wanted to do things their own way, and they did."

Chapter 15: Love and Loathing in Las Vegas

A loud and clear BBC-quality British voice filled the hotel mini-ballroom: *"Ella and her dad!"*

I started to get up, but Ella wouldn't budge from the seat next to me. We were at The Mirage hotel in Las Vegas, drawn by the dual lure of the Beatles "Love" Cirque du Soleil spectacular and first-ever Fest for Beatles Fans in Sin City.

"Ella and her dad will be up after the next act."

The room was packed for the Beatles sound-alike contest, a Fest staple and always one of my favorite parts of the weekend. Dozens of folks screw up their courage to perform a Beatles song, either alone or as part of a duo. A handful of finalists get to play later that night before thousands jammed in the grand ballroom. The winner or winners, picked by the applause from the throngs, earn prizes – Beatles posters and other memorabilia – and the acclamation of fellow fans.

I'd never summoned the nerve to get up and do a song. My guitar playing was nothing to be ashamed of – I'd played in a band or two in high school, and would jam occasionally with friends into my adulthood. I was terrified, though, of singing, at least in front of strangers. But I had a secret weapon: Ella.

At age 10, she was on her way to becoming an accomplished bass player. Ella's teacher, jazzman Wayne Roberts, threw in some familiar tunes to help keep her engaged as he took her through scales and classical pieces. He started her off with the simple "Love Me Do," built up to "I've Just Seen a Face," and, amazingly, to "Dear Prudence," one of the hardest and perhaps the best of the McCartney Beatle bass lines.

I was most charmed, though, by Ella's ability to play "For No One," a deep cut from "Revolver" in which Paul maturely melded pop and classical influences. Ella practiced it constantly, singing along while playing the bass – no mean feat for a musician of any age. And when she found she couldn't quite hit a couple notes to her satisfaction, she transposed the song from the key of C to G, with an ease that astounded me. I could thump out a rudimentary version on piano, though changing the key was far harder for me. I eventually adjusted and we'd play the song together in our living room, her voice lending sweetness to a wistful tune, and her bass work McCartney note-perfect.

I'd gotten it my head that we'd play "For No One" together at the sound-alike tryouts. I was confident the combination of a relatively obscure fan favorite, played on a McCartney Hofner knockoff bass and sung by a 10-year-old Little Ms. Sunshine look-alike would be enough, to catapult me – I mean us – to the big stage.

"We're waiting for Ella and her dad!"

Ella had said she would consider my duet idea. But now, she was tired and a little feverish. I was flushed as well, attributing my discomfort – and hers – to spending too much time in the 110-degree Las Vegas sun. Even in dry heat, it was foolish to walk up and down The Strip in daylight amid wind gusts that felt like furnace blasts.

I grabbed Ella's left arm and pulled as she clutched her bass to her chest and transformed into a statue. "Come on," I said. "Let's go."

"Last call for Ella and her dad!"

"We've got to get up there now or we're going to lose our turn!" I told Ella, as the emcee, Martin Lewis, an internationally known Beatle expert, British TV personality and Fest mainstay, looked around the room for us.

There were dozens of other people waiting to play. We'd already been in the room for more than 90 minutes, watching renditions of Beatle songs by performers ranging from near-professional quality musicians to others, like me, who should have limited their singing to the shower.

"Are Ella and her dad here?"

"I don't want to do this," Ella said.

"But you said you would. We've been practicing."

"I never said I would – you said we would. I don't feel good."

"But we'll be up there for two minutes, it will be no time at all."

She turned to Theresa. "He's not listening to me. Will you tell him?"

"She's not feeling well. Maybe we can come back later and try again."

"There's no later. Come on, Ella, let's do this."

"I'm not doing this," she said.

"You said you wanted to."

"No, you said *you* wanted to."

"It's not for me, it's for you."

"No," she said, turning away from me before staring down at the carpet. "It's for you."

"Final call for Ella and her dad!"

"This is ridiculous," Theresa said. "I'm going up there to tell him you're not doing this and to move on."

"You know," I told Ella, as her mother marched to the front of the room, "you blew an opportunity."

"Go to hell," she said, standing up, slinging her bass gig sack over her shoulder before storming past a long line of sound-alike wannabes and out the back door.

I was stunned – not so much because she'd just told me to go to hell for the first time, but because her tone was more disappointment than anger. Theresa chased after Ella, but not before giving me a profane comeuppance.

As Martin moved on to the next act, I sat alone, if not in a mini-hell, then in a purgatory of my own creation. Las Vegas can bring out the worst in some people. I'm not a gambler. I like an occasional drink, but there was no danger of any kind of drunken binge here, if only because there was no way I would pay $15 a pop for a cocktail. But in Las Vegas I emerged – or exposed myself – as the creature I vowed never to become: the Bad Beatle Dad.

Like the road to hell, our path to Las Vegas was paved with the usual good intentions. The Cirque du Soleil "Love" show appeared custom made for us: a family-friendly Beatles spectacular that combined music and elements of theater, our other primary avocation. Ella saw her first Broadway show – "The Music Man" – at age 4 ("Hey, are they stealing a Beatles song?" she whispered as Marian the Librarian sang "Till There Was You," a tune the group famously covered).

I'd been a fan of Cirque du Soleil since the late 1980s when I was assigned to cover the French Canadian troupe's New York debut. I spent a couple days with the performers and crew as they pitched a tent and set up camp on a then-empty lot in Lower Manhattan, with views of the Statue of Liberty.

George kicked off the "Love" project, shortly before his death, with his friend, Cirque du Soleil creator Guy Laliberte. Reports of using Beatles remixes for the show's soundtrack were troubling. But George Martin's son, Giles, would be working with his dad on the effort, keeping it all in the Beatle family. The early tracks we'd heard were inspiring, and respectful of the music. They'd be played in a specially built theater with a state-of-the-art sound system.

We'd started our Vegas jaunt on a bittersweet note. Charles had organized a trip to see "Love" that past winter, and a handful of our Liverpool tour mates went, including Brooklyn Ed, with whom we'd spent the most recent Fest. He'd called us soon after the Fest with an extra ticket to a show by the Beatles tribute act 1964 at Carnegie Hall. But none of us could go because Ella was performing that night with her chorus.

We also couldn't go to see "Love" with Charles, Ed and the gang. The timing, thanks to school schedules, kept us tethered to Brooklyn. We wound up being both glad and sad we didn't go: The sprinkler system apparently malfunctioned mid-show, dousing the audience and stopping the performance. Far, far worse, Brooklyn Ed took ill soon after and never made it home. Theresa represented us at his memorial service, where friends remembered him as a creative soul who embraced life even as his health waned. Part of our unspoken mission was to complete the trip Ed was unable to finish.

The bird's-eye view of the Grand Canyon shortly before we landed in Vegas awed Theresa and Ella, whose oohs and ahs were echoed by other passengers. I didn't look – peeking out the windows of planes only heightened my high anxiety. My senses would soon be overwhelmed by our drive up The Strip, a visual cacophony of a neon Stonehenge whose impressiveness, I decided, barely outweighed its cheesiness.

Our hotel, two imposing obelisk buildings that seemed to part in the middle, flexing like the spine of an open book, appeared sedate and welcoming in comparison to some of the gaudier surroundings. Most inviting was the orange-and-yellow "Love" logo, with silhouettes of the Beatles, splashed across the top of the complex's dual wings.

We thought we knew what to expect from movie and TV depictions of Vegas. But nothing prepared us for going from stifling heat to freezing air-conditioning, and the constant *ping-ping-ping* of the gaming floor with flashing lights that would have sent even The Who's Tommy fleeing to the refuge of a sensory deprivation tank.

After checking into our room, we walked around – but not directly through the gaming floor, a no-no with a minor – and checked out the "Love" lobby, near the entrance to the theater. We'd watched on TV the week before as plaques honoring John and George were dedicated there with Paul, Ringo and Yoko on hand to mark the show's first anniversary. Only feet away were slot machines topped by the Beatles "Love" logo. It can be a dangerous game guessing what John and George would have thought about that, but I hope they would have found some mordant humor in the unsettling juxtaposition.

We had tickets for a performance later that evening, so we grabbed a quick bite at the California Pizza Kitchen in the hotel. We returned to find a long line of excited folks – among them many families. The theater impressed us: plush seats, each quipped with speakers. I justified getting the cheap seats that put us in the second-to-last row. "From here, we can see everything, including the audience, which may be the best part of the show," I reasoned, though Theresa and Ella, as usual, weren't buying it.

The theater went dark as "Because," a cappella, filled the auditorium. Goosebumps covered me and I saw them rise on Ella and Theresa's arms. It's a cliché to say it sounded like the Beatles were in the room with us. But as I closed my eyes, I could see John,

George and Paul sitting in a semi-circle at Abbey Road, during one of their last recording sessions, singing and re-singing John's Yoko-and-Beethoven-inspired gem, adding layers of lush, yet razor-sharp harmony.

Then the stage exploded into a combination of "Yellow Submarine" and Mr. Kite's circus come to life, with acrobats flying via wires and trampolines to a familiar soundtrack that dreamily weaved from "A Hard Day's Night" to the drum solo from "The End" to "Get Back," each snippet fading into another. The show tantalized, like a live performance of a 3-D movie, daring you to reach out and touch – no more so than during a moment of shadow play in which performers miming the Beatles engaged in a "conversation" pieced together from scraps of recording studio banter. Though the moment is fleeting, it's clear from the shadowy figures which Beatle is which – a sign of just how ingrained the images of John, Paul, George and Ringo are in us.

While the "cameo" is touching, there's a certain eeriness attached even as the audience wants the illusion to go on. "I can sum up the show in three words," I said, as we left with an audience that somehow was ecstatic and speechless at the same time. "Nothing is real."

"Does that mean you liked it or didn't like it?" Theresa asked.

"I think I liked it."

"Me, too," Ella said.

"I thought it was pretty damn amazing," Theresa said. "Though I would have liked it a lot more if we had better seats. Life's too short to skimp on things you like. Don't be such a cheap bastard."

"Bastard." That also was the last word Theresa hurled over her shoulder at me the next day as she chased after Ella when she fled the sound-alike tryouts. I stayed for a while before wandering out and around to the rest of the Fest. Former Wings members Lawrence Juber, Denny Seiwell and Denny Laine spoke and played. So did Peter and Gordon – Peter Asher and Gordon Waller – the British pop duo inextricably tied to the Beatles through song (they recorded several Lennon-McCartney tunes, most notably "World Without Love") and life (Paul nearly married Peter's sister, actress Jane Asher, and wrote the melody for "Yesterday" while living with the Asher family).

But I was most thrilled by the talk given by Victor Spinetti, the British actor who appeared in "A Hard Day's Night" (as the fussy TV director), "Help!" (as the bumbling mad scientist) and "Magical Mystery Tour" (as the screaming military man). Spinetti was the guest of honor at my first Fest in 1981. The born raconteur told the same stories, got the same laughs and cheers in the same places, transporting me back to one of my first pure Beatle experiences.

After wowing the Vegas crowd, Spinetti went to the lobby area outside the main ballroom, where he was mobbed for autographs, including by teenagers about my age when I'd first seen him more than a quarter-century earlier. I wished Theresa, and especially, Ella, were here for this. I felt ashamed for ruining what should have been a fun time building new stories – which, like Spinetti's tales of the Beatles, would wear well with the years, if only in our family lore.

I decided to go upstairs to our room, make amends and coax the girls out to watch the sound-alike finals. As I arrived at the elevator bank, the doors opened to reveal Ella carrying her bass and Theresa holding my acoustic guitar and our Beatles songbook. "She's feeling better," Theresa said. "Let's find a place where we can play. Just the three of us."

We settled in a corner of the lobby area, sat and started going through our songbook, starting with "I Will," one of Theresa's favorites. We played softly – Ella's bass wasn't amplified. But as we looked up after the final chord, a crowd started to form around us. The gathering grew, with people calling out favorite numbers and singing along. A man in his 20s with a tambourine joined in. He looked eerily liked Christopher Walken. Between songs, we learned he talked just like Christopher Walken. He claimed to be Christopher Walken's son (I looked him up later – he's not, but it's his shtick). No matter – the tambourine attracted even more people.

Before we knew it, there were dozens, including a family from New Mexico with a daughter and son, no older than 5 and 7, clad in homemade Sgt. Pepper outfits. A radio host from Japan invited us to come on his weekly Beatles show if we ever found ourselves in Tokyo. A well-dressed Persian man who opened a wallet stuffed with $100 bills to give us his card, invited us to stay at his mansion in San Francisco. "I love the Beatles!" he gushed. "I love this family!"

Soon after, the sound-alike finals ended in the

main ballroom, and scores more Fest revelers poured in the lobby, among them musicians with guitars, basses and amps. One guy even lugged a small drum kit. Hotel security guards, dressed like Secret Service agents and equipped with the requisite earpieces, left the gaming floor and tried to break up the party. But they were outshouted, and soon gave up. Some even began helping run extension chords to power the amps. Spinetti, wearing a white ascot and a black baseball cap emblazoned with the Nike swoosh, returned to the lobby, sat, clapped and sang along.

A thirtyish bass player saw Ella plucking away, and suggested she plug into his amp for a number. "What do you want to play?" he asked.

"How about, 'I've Just Seen a Face?'" she said. "I play it in A."

The guitarists were bunched in small groups throughout. One strummer turned to me and said, "I'm going to do the low Paul harmony, you take the high Paul harmony on the 'Falling' chorus."

I nodded, but I had no idea what he was talking about. The song kicked off. I closed my eyes, listened and heard the harmony in my head. When the chorus arrived, I opened my mouth, and something approaching Paul's double-tracked high harmony tumbled out. As I sang, I glanced toward Ella, who sat cross-legged as she played her part perfectly, earning cheers when the song ended.

What happened in Vegas would not stay there. We'd take it with us. I'd been a jerk, but at least maybe I learned how to listen. Which I showed, in a modest way, the next day when I gave in to Theresa and El-la's pleas to skip the crowded airport shuttle bus. It killed me, but we splurged on a cab to the airport amid weather reports calling for temperatures hitting a record 115 degrees.

"This was all very nice," Ella said during our ride, as The Strip gave way to The Desert. "But if we're going to spend this kind of money, I'd rather be in Liverpool."

Chapter 16: Get Back

The letters' arrivals were heralded by the neat, compact British-style cursive that invariably spurred a double take as I'd pluck them out of our mailbox. The handwriting, reminiscent of the familiar scrawl of my late Glasgow-reared grandmother, took me back to the birthday cards, packed with a crisp five-dollar bill, I'd eagerly await from her each July. The return address on the more recent letters – 10 Admiral Grove – heralded a gift of another sort from the most memorable friend we made in Liverpool.

Margaret's letters to Ella inevitably started with an apology for not writing back sooner, blaming, variously, cataracts and a busy schedule that included dealing not only with her own family, but with knocks on her door by visitors from around the world. Surprise guests included Ringo's daughter Leigh and son, Zak. "He's a drummer, too," Margaret relayed. "He said he plays with a group called 'The Who.'"

Ella wrote regularly, telling Margaret about school, the latest "Harry Potter" book she'd read – and meeting Paul, enclosing a newspaper clipping and a photo. "How wonderful for you!" Margaret wrote back.

The letters, filled with the ordinary and occasional sprinkles of the extraordinary, reinforced our memories of Liverpool as a homey, down-to-earth city with more than its share of magic – and reminded us of our own blessings. Margaret would refer to Ella as "my American granddaughter" and send holiday cards. Her occasional notes connected us to the Beatles and their hometown in a way that even meeting Paul never could. Her missives also made us long for a return to Liverpool.

But that would be hard to justify, financially and otherwise. Especially the otherwise. I wasn't sure we could take the inevitable teasing from family, friends and co-workers for whom our Beatles obsession provided fodder for humor – and concern. One close family friend went as far as to decry us "bad parents" because we never took Ella to Disneyworld (hey, she didn't like rides, and her tastes ran more to Rocky Raccoon than Mickey Mouse). Uttered even partially in jest, that hurt, mostly because of the implication we were raising our daughter to be a freak. We fretted occasionally about that, too.

But our consciences were clear: At age 11, Ella was an honor student about to graduate from a challenging public elementary school program. She was a child with a good sense of humor and plenty of friends her own age (and, okay, more than a few quite a bit older). She appeared reasonably well adjusted, and very much her own person, even if she, like her parents, possessed some quirks.

We also could justify, to ourselves, if not others, her life-long Beatle brainwashing by noting Ella's increasing musical accomplishments, which had grown exponentially since meeting Paul. Her vocal skills, honed through the Brooklyn Youth Chorus, and her devotion to the bass – first on bass guitar, then learning classical technique on the upright bass – helped her get into one of the city's elite public middle schools, which she was set to attend in the fall. But her heart still brought her back to the Beatles and rock and roll.

In 2006, not long before CBGB closed, Ella and I jammed into the famed punk club for a School of Rock Beatles show featuring our young pals, brothers Damon and Brendan Smith. I expected to see kids pounding drums, slapping basses and strumming guitars with varying degrees of proficiency. What I didn't expect was the horn section as the first crew of kids took to the modest stage for a startlingly strong version of "Sgt. Pepper's Lonely Hearts Club Band."

Ella turned to me. "They're playing it the right way!" she said, as surprised as I was.

The song kicked off a greatest hits show featuring a couple dozen kids, eight to 18, moving on and off the stage, like clockwork under the direction of pro musicians nicknamed Pinky and Tomato. The older, more accomplished students not only mixed well with the kids just learning their first chords, but served as guides, helping the little ones plug in and tune up. That proved even more impressive than the kick-ass version of "Back in the USSR."

"Do you think I could do that?" Ella asked me afterward, as we squeezed out of the clammy club onto the Bowery.

She wasn't asking if Theresa and I would let her join the School of Rock as much as whether I thought she was capable. We were thrilled by her interest, though she was still shy about performing and had yet to reach a level of confidence equal to her skills. We were ready to sign her up at any time, though she occasionally wavered – my moronic Vegas stunt certainly hadn't helped.

She finally girded herself to take up the challenge, and within weeks climbed onto the stage of Crash Mansion, another Bowery club, laying down the funky bassline on Archie Bell and The Drells' "Tighten Up," and surprising all with clear, powerful vocals on a duet with an older, bass-thumping girl on "I Want You Back."

"Damn, how does such a big voice come out of such a little girl?" I overheard one woman remark to another.

I wondered the same thing.

Ella's self-assurance grew not only with performing, but from learning to successfully juggle her increasingly packed calendar of lessons and practices with school, and from making friends with similar musical interests. If she ever felt like an oddball with parents more likely to take her to the Cavern Club than Cinderella's Castle, she was right at home at the delightfully chaotic School of Rock, where a mural featuring The Ramones and Run-DMC competed for wall space with posters from past shows celebrating the likes of The Who, Led Zeppelin and the Beatles.

The money we gladly spent on Ella's growing musical extracurricular activities, though, didn't get us any closer to another Beatles vacation – or any other kind of major getaway. I was making a good living at my new job, but still pulling in considerably less than my old salary. Theresa recently had sold half of her Music Together business, which meant less income. The bulk of the proceeds went toward producing a musical – about the Statue of Liberty – she became determined to bring to the New York stage.

Meeting Paul had inspired us to follow our dreams. But, as we knew from the Beatles' story, it takes hard work and sacrifices to make great things happen, though with no guarantee of success.

Amid our busy days, Liverpool beckoned – in Margaret's letters, in the "Liverpool '08" poster hanging in our basement, in the emails from Charles touting the upcoming Beatles Week as the biggest and best ever amid Liverpool's crowning as that year's European Capital of Culture. The most compelling tug, though, after our nothing-is-real partial misadventure in Las Vegas, was a craving for a return to a pure Beatles experience.

Ella reminded me of what I told her when Theresa and I convinced her to stop crying and meet Paul: "You only regret the things you don't do."

Smart (smart-ass) kid – still two years from being a teenager and already using her father's words against him.

We started to look into how we could make the trip on the cheap. We'd skip the London half of Charles' tour. We'd exhaust our credit card points to pay for airfare. We'd forgo souvenirs – no exceptions. We'd ensure that we'd visit places we'd missed the last time by planning ahead. We wouldn't go if we couldn't secure tours of John and Paul's homes.

Since our last trip, Liverpool finally caught up with the Internet and we were able to make some reservations. Through the miracle of Google Maps, I sketched out itineraries that would fill our days with long walks through the Beatles' Liverpool, costing us little more than some rubber sole from our sneakers. Sure, we wanted to check out the music scene, but didn't need the full-access wristbands we'd purchased in 2005. We emailed Charles and explained our situation. His reply made it a go: "We can work it out!"

As Theresa, Ella and I packed with our tour mates in the living room of John's boyhood home at 251 Menlove Avenue – the two-story, semi-detached cottage-style house where his Aunt Mimi raised him – we could almost see the ghosts among us. Perhaps it was just our imagination, sparked by the surreal experience of standing somewhere we'd long seen only in our mind's eye – a place, thanks to word-pictures painted in the best of the biographies, felt like something out of our own childhoods.

There was a 1940s-style radio, much like the one John's Uncle George snaked a wire from through the ceiling to a pillow speaker in his nephew's closet of a bedroom upstairs. The wire carried the siren call of American rock and roll broadcast in the dead of night. There was the picture window where Mimi would sit, peering out, impatiently waiting for John to arrive home, from school, from long nights out, from Germany after he came home the first time from Hamburg in defeat. There was the plaque John had made with

Mimi's famous (at least among Beatles fans) words: "The guitar's all right John, but you'll never make a living out of it."

Yes, we could see ghosts everywhere. But we didn't expect to hear them.

From the cramped vestibule, where Mimi would make John and Paul rehearse nose-to-nose so they didn't disturb her, emanated "Please Please Me," in two-part harmony – albeit one part at a time. I peeked into the space, not much bigger than two old-school phone booths welded together, to find our tour mate, a fellow New Yorker who goes by the name Dave Jay.

Dave performs a largely improvised, one-man Beatles show, ably imitating all four, playing songs and answering questions from the audience in the voices (and based on his impressive knowledge, what likely might have been the words) of John, Paul, George and Ringo. He brought his by turns comic and poignant quadrophenic act to Liverpool for International Beatles Week. But at this moment, he was in split-personality glory, trading off harmonies as John and Paul on a song John wrote in the tiny room upstairs, decorated with pictures of Elvis and Brigitte Bardot.

"This is where it happened," Dave said, the sun peaking through the vestibule's stained-glass windows, and shining onto his wonder-filled eyes. "It all happened *right here!*"

He gushed about his inner and outer harmony as we filed back onto our bus, which took us to 20 Forthlin Road, where Paul moved with his family in the mid-1950s. It's about a half-hour walk from Mendips, a route John and Paul traversed many times, on foot and bike, as they became friends and musical partners. But even from the inside of the bus, more than 50 years after they met, we could see the changes as we crossed from Woolton to Allerton.

John's neighborhood is leafy and suburban, near a golf course, and, of course, the sprawling Strawberry Field. Other than the modern-day cars whizzing by and satellite dishes topping many roofs, it probably looks as much as it did in his boyhood. The area certainly was far less hardscrabble than the sections of Liverpool where the other Beatles were raised – even if, amid lingering post-war deprivation and the death of John's Uncle George, Aunt Mimi took in university students as borders to make ends meet.

Paul's final Liverpool home, at 20 Forthlin Road, is a pleasant, if modest, cookie-cutter government council flat that the McCartneys were lucky to get. As story goes in Liverpool, they were nudged to the top of the list because Paul's mother, Mary, was a beloved local nurse. Behind the home is a police academy that includes a field where police dogs are trained. A visit by Princess Diana to the facility is a local point of pride.

We were greeted at the ivy-covered front gate by the red-brick house's live-in caretaker, John Haliday, who sported an impish McCartney-like grin, if only because he knew what we all were thinking. "My God, he looks just like him," Theresa whispered.

"No, I'm not related," John declared pre-emp-tively, in a surprisingly cheerful voice, considering he likely gets the question from the 20 or so tour groups he meets every week.

After squirreling our cameras away in a cupboard – Britain's National Trust, which runs both homes, doesn't allow pictures inside either building – John escorted us into Paul's living room, complete with a piano, much like the one Jim McCartney would bang out jazz tunes on to entertain his wife and sons, Paul and Mike.

The history of the house, though, is tinged with sorrow. Mary McCartney became ill shortly after the family moved in and died of cancer about a year later, when Paul was just 14. But the abode, while decidedly humble, has a homier feel than the posher Mendips. Paul's pals always were welcome in the living room at 20 Forthlin Road, where they'd listen to the latest pop records and learn the new tunes. He and John wrote early Beatles songs – most notably, "I Saw Her Standing There" – where we were now standing.

Upstairs, Paul's small bedroom overlooks the field where the police dogs are trained. Our guide, John, said his family took him to a police dog show on July 6, 1957, skipping the Woolton Fete, where the Quaryman played the day Lennon met McCartney. Not all that long before our visit, John said, neighbors reported that Paul showed up alone at the house one day and knocked on the door – but John wasn't home. But he did meet Paul once – around 1968, a few years after the Beatles last visited Liverpool as a group. A teenage John found Paul alone in a local park with his dog sheepdog Martha (the inspiration for "Martha, My Dear").

Like Mendips, most of the furniture is from the period, but not original to the house. The recreation works better at Forthlin Road, though, thanks to the guide provided by the many pictures snapped in the 1950s and 1960s by Mike McCartney. Some of the photos now decorate the walls of 20 Forthlin Road. The most famous shot is probably the black-and-white portrait of Paul in the modest backyard, as seen on the cover of his great 2005 "Chaos and Creation in the Backyard" album. The picture shows a pensive, apparently teenage Paul, guitar in hand as he sits in a canvas folding chair, peering beyond the wash flapping above him on the clothes line.

As we filed into the backyard, our group scrambled toward the canvas chair planted on the same spot as on the album cover. John gamely snapped pictures as we took turns sitting. "It's not the chair in the picture," he said. "But I won't tell anybody."

We wouldn't have to settle for replacement furniture the next morning as we traveled about 4.5 miles from Liverpool's City Centre northeast to what can only be described as a Beatles time capsule. Our TARDIS wasn't a British police call box, but rather a black cab that took us from the Adelphi to a neighborhood called Derby (pronounced "Darby"). As much as we were trying to keep down the expenses, the cab was a necessity. We couldn't find a direct public bus and we didn't know what to expect in terms of neighborhood safety. Besides, the morning drizzle quickly turned into a driving rain.

We slowly filed out of the cab after arriving at the leafy street called Hayman's Green. As I wiped the rain from Ella's and my glasses, I wondered whether we were in the right place on the quiet block of nice, generally well-kept Victorian homes, until I spotted the circa-1960 Coca-Cola sign affixed to the side of 8 Hayman's Green. Under the familiar red-and-white logo were these words in green type: "CASBAH Coffee Club."

We were about 15 minutes early for the tour we'd reserved online weeks before. The three of us clamored to the front door and rang the bell. A gruff voice blaring from the intercom directed us to the back of the house, where we joined waiting tourists from Japan, Germany and Argentina under an overhang as we tried to dodge unusually large, grape-like raindrops.

Nobody seemed to mind the English rain as we made small talk. Everybody there had been told by fellow Beatles fans that this was the must-do stop in Liverpool: the club started by Pete Best's mother, Mona, in her family's basement, the spot where Beatlemania began to take hold on its smallest, most primitive level in 1959. John, Paul and George met Pete at the Casbah, beginning one of the more bittersweet chapters in the group's history.

The club closed in 1962, not long before Ringo replaced Pete and the Beatles scored their first hit with "Love Me Do." The Casbah stayed shuttered until 2006 when Pete and his brothers, Rory and Roag, began giv-

ing tours, marking a huge step in Pete's gradual em-
bracement of his role in Beatles history. We'd seen
him a couple of times at The Fest For Beatles Fans. He
seemed both a shy and friendly man, who forced himself to become a raconteur, telling stories from the old
days. He seemed most at ease playing drums with his
Pete Best Band, whose repertoire includes songs Liverpool groups played in Hamburg in the late 1950s and
1960s, and new tunes that sound like they came from
that era.

The Casbah hadn't yet re-opened when we'd
last visited Liverpool. The most memorable mention of
Pete on that trip came when we passed the employment center where he worked for years on our way
back from visiting Liverpool John Lennon Airport
(motto: "Above us only sky").

The skies above us were weeping when Rory
Best mercifully opened the back door a few minutes
before tour time and let us in. We walked into a dark,
damp space that emanated an ancient, stuffy must
contained by the concrete walls. "We're breathing the
same stale air as the Beatles," Theresa quipped, part in
wonder, part sarcastically.

It wasn't the large, open space I'd been expecting, but rather a warren of small rooms that spilled one
into the next. Rory told us the basement was supposed
to hold about 300, which was hard to imagine. But
when the Beatles played, "They must have had about
500 girls down here, screaming, shouting, crying," he
said.

Before they were the Beatles, the Quarrymen came around when the Casbah was about to open and cheekily demanded to be put on the bill. But they'd have to help get the club into shape before they could play. "Mona put them to work," Rory said.

Paul painted an elaborate spider's web, white on the black wall, with a red spider at the center. The future Cynthia Lennon painted a silver silhouette of John, playing his guitar in a stylish crouch, on the wall. They all painted stars of varying sizes on the ceiling. The art works were all there, untouched, along with ancient amplifiers and microphones, and a battered old piano – a hand-me-down from Quarryman Ken Brown's family. "McCartney's played it thousands of times," Rory said in almost an aside.

Unlike many of the other Beatles attractions we'd visited, this wasn't anything like a museum, though there was one glass display case whose treasures included a strangely familiar trophy. Rory said the trophy is the one pictured on the cover of "Sgt. Pepper's Lonely Heart's Club Band," near the flower-made "L" in Beatles. He said John simply rang up Mona one day and asked to borrow it, which seemed bizarre, given none of the Beatles ever spoke to Pete after they made Brian Epstein fire him from the band five years earlier.

The trophy story underscored for us Liverpool's hold on the group and the ties that aren't often talked about, but inextricably bind them to their hometown. The late Neil Aspinall, who rose from the Beatles' van driver to the head of Apple, fathered Pete and Rory's half-brother Roag as a teenager, during an affair with his pals' mum while living with the Bests. Rory, of course, didn't mention that during his tour, which brimmed more with a mater-of-fact familiarity with the young Beatles than with bitterness.

We broke our "no souvenir" rule, buying a book written and signed by the Best brothers, and T-shirts – including one with a reproduction of Cynthia's silhouette of John.

The skies cleared a little over an hour later as we exited the Casbah and returned to 2008. As we readjusted our eyes from dim to daylight, we were forced to look at the Beatles in yet another unexpected way. "That place didn't look much different than our basement," Ella noted. "Though ours isn't that big."

"It doesn't look a lot different than *anybody's* basement," Theresa added.

On Rory's advice, we walked a couple blocks to a main road and hailed a cab. But instead of returning to the Adelphi, we headed to Strawberry Field. I'd mapped out a route that would take us on our own walking tour from Strawberry Field to Penny Lane, from the A-side to the B-side of perhaps the Beatles' most memorable – and most personal – single. We'd have lunch in Penny Lane before visiting Margaret, who was expecting us that afternoon.

But not long into our journey, the blue suburban skies turned gray and reopened with a vengeance. We huddled under the one small umbrella we had between us, and stutter-stepped our way slowly along the sidewalk. Somewhere early on, not far from John's house, we took the wrong turn along Allerton Road and wandered about 20 minutes before realizing we were hopelessly lost. Tempers became short as bladders – and hunger – grew.

The term "cheap bastard" was hurled at me more than once, and Google Maps was cursed with even more vehemence. By this point, I would have been glad to pay for another taxi, but the few that passed us were occupied. We couldn't find a bus, which was odd, since all routes led to Penny Lane. The sidewalks were empty, without a local to be found that rain-drenched weekday morning. "Can't we just go back to the hotel?" Ella growled.

We couldn't. We'd made a date with Margaret. Besides, we had no way of quickly returning to the Adelphi if we (all) wanted to. I finally buttonholed a cabbie stopped at a traffic signal and got directions to the bus. It's only about 1.5 miles from Strawberry Field to Penny Lane, but we'd lost about an hour and added a mile to the trip with our wet wanderings.

We got off the bus near the Penny Lane Woolworth's, the one where Cynthia worked behind the counter, the one where Paul bought his combs. We went in to purchase a box of chocolates for Margaret – and find ourselves some paper towels to dry off. We wolfed down Tex-Mex wraps at a nearby restaurant, and walked to the middle of the roundabout. Only we didn't need a shelter – the rain had stopped. We did need a cab.

Even I agreed that we wouldn't take chance

on walking for the final, and most important leg of the day's journey. We fairly quickly hailed a taxi and hopped in. "10 Admiral Row, please," I said

The driver turned and looked at me in confusion. "Come again?" he asked.

Was he playing a game with a hapless tourist? No, I quickly realized: I'd bungled the address, getting it mixed up with a spot in Brooklyn.

"Aw, just bring us to Ringo's house."

The hack left us off at the corner of Admiral Grove, not near where Ringo's mum worked as a barmaid, but the opposite side, at the far end of the block. As we walked past the tiny, well-kept houses, I thought about how the first time I came here nearly 18 years ago to the day, I was an intruder. The second time, 15 years later, I was a moderately well-behaved tourist. Now, I came with my family – as a guest.

Ella beat us to the door and knocked. Margaret opened the door and her arms, folding Ella into a hug. Ella, I noticed, was now as tall as Margaret, who beckoned us inside to sit in the tiny living room, a cozy fit for the four of us.

"How are you doing in school? You'll be doing very well, are you?" Margaret asked Ella. "I have trouble with me eyes, which is why I haven't wrote to you."

As she told us about her optical travails ("I had my cataracts done and one of them went wrong") and her family, there was a knock on the door. I looked through the window at Margaret's request. It was a group of tourists, apparently from Japan. Margaret didn't answer the door. I felt bad. There could be a Japanese family as crazy about the Beatles as we are leaving in disappointment. "They can come back later. They always do," Margaret said. "We have fun and games here, you know."

She showed Ella her doll collection, and broke out the chocolates and some biscuits. She told us about the many knocks on her door, recounting the recent visit from Ringo's daughter and son, and recalling how Ringo's mum would pop by to sit in her old living room.

As we chatted, I got up and looked at the pictures that filled her walls – there were even more than when we last visited. Pictures of Margaret's beloved Elvis. Photos of Cilla Black, who rose from cloakroom girl at the Cavern to become a star. Among the pictures, not far from a shot of Margaret and Ringo, was the photo of Ella and Paul we had sent Margaret.

"People always say, 'We always talk about these people, you actually met them,'" Margaret said, looking at Ella. They shared a nod that turned to a knowing smile.

Chapter 17: While You're Busy Making Other Plans

As I walked hand-in-hand with Ella past the Dakota in the early December chill, just over two months after she met Paul, memory transported me back 25 years to 1980.

It was 11:30 p.m., and a school night. But that didn't stop my younger brother, Drew, and I from our weeknight ritual of secreting ourselves in his room, huddled around the new 12-inch black-and-white Zenith TV bought with $59 saved from confirmation presents (his) and eight-grade graduation gifts (mine) at Crazy Eddie's. With the volume turned down to a whisper, we waited for "Prisoner Cell Block H" to begin on Channel 11. "Prisoner Cell Block H" was a 1970s unintentionally campy Australian soap opera about a women's prison – a kind of babe-behind-bars romp, but far bigger on the laughs than the babes. At 14, this passed for titillation.

Drew's room – it used to be our room, until about a year earlier when I got my own space in our semi-finished basement – was about the size of a prison cell itself. It felt even smaller as we flanked the tiny screen, not breathing so we could hear every word of overheated dialogue. We had to be careful not to wake our mother and younger sister, sleeping in adjoining rooms, lest we infuriate our father who was not to be interrupted in the downstairs living room as he watched "The Tonight Show" – especially not during

Johnny Carson's monologue.

We were a few minutes into the latest jailhouse melodrama when words to this effect crawled across the bottom of the screen: "A man tentatively identified as former Beatle John Lennon has been reported shot on the Upper West Side and rushed to Roosevelt Hospital."

I was a kid, with no inkling I would wind up a journalist. But I already possessed some news instincts, probably from reading newspapers, magazines or watching TV most of my waking moments, which were many, since I was a teenage insomniac.

I knew the 11 p.m. news broadcasts were over. CNN was about six months old – not that we had it. Our working-class corner of Brooklyn wouldn't be wired for cable for years. Besides, my raised-on-radio, Depression-born parents wouldn't do anything as foolish as pay for TV (they didn't give in until 2008).

But I knew ABC's "Monday Night Football" was still on. So we left the latest battle of wills between prisoner leader Bea and hard-ass guard Vera (the girls called her "vinegar tits," which made us giggle like the schoolboys were) and flipped over to Channel 7.

The words "tentatively identified" and the lack of the word "dead" gave me some optimism as the dial clicked four times under my hand. Howard Cosell quickly dashed those hopes, somberly delivering the news of what had transpired barely an hour earlier.

"Remember, this is just a football game, no matter who wins or loses," Cosell began in his world-famous, voice-of-authority nasal tones. "An unspeakable tragedy confirmed to us by ABC News in New York City: John Lennon, outside of his apartment building on the West Side of New York City, the most famous, perhaps, of all the Beatles, shot twice in the back, rushed to Roosevelt Hospital, dead on arrival."

I grabbed my brother's half of our Beatles record collection and pounded downstairs past my father, still in his mailman's uniform, eating dinner off the tray table in front of his Archie Bunker-like easy chair. "What the hell are you doing?" he shouted, irked at the interruption.

"Somebody shot John Lennon," I said, burying the lead. "He's dead."

"Oh," my father replied, taking his attention off "The Tonight Show" for just a moment. "Well, it's too damn late to play any records. Go to sleep!"

I continued onto to my basement room. I wouldn't play any records. I certainly wouldn't turn on my TV – it was a circa-1960, 19-inch black-and-white Zenith my father found in the garbage while on the job, and hauled to our house in his mail truck. The TV worked – kind of: The image would progressively narrow to a white dot every 20 minutes or so. A well-placed slap to the right side of the metal unit would bring the full screen back, albeit temporarily.

I jumped into bed and turned on my clock radio, which had not only AM and FM, but audio feeds of TV stations. Most nights when I couldn't sleep, I would tune into Larry King's overnight radio show, taking a break around 2 a.m. to catch back-to-back repeats of "The Mary Tyler Moore Show," making sure I kept the

volume down on my makeshift pillow speaker, lest my
father stomp on the floor, occasionally sending dirt flying through cracks in the tin ceiling onto my face.

I flipped from radio station to radio station –
WPLJ, WNEW, WABC – listening to the DJs struggle
with their emotions, field calls from weeping fans and
play John's music, including solo tracks I then barely
knew. Meanwhile, fans massed outside the Dakota,
where John had lived and died, brandishing candles
and singing his songs.

I wanted to be there. But there was no question I would be staying put. My father usually stayed
up through Tom Snyder's "Tomorrow Show," which
didn't end until 2 a.m. I wasn't going to sneak out of
the house in the middle of the night and take a train to
a place I wasn't even sure how to find. Not in 1980 New
York. Not at 14.

I didn't fall asleep until about 6 a.m. When my
mother woke me up for school about an hour later, I
told her I was sick, which was only vaguely a lie. I felt,
in the same instant, a huge lump and a gnawing emp-
tiness in the pit of my stomach. I wanted to cry, but
didn't know how. I was heartsick.

The Daily News' headline in the Dec. 9 edition was: "John Lennon Shot Here." There was a short
piece inside, written almost like any other crime story
– probably attributable mostly to the late hour, and
partly to a failure to realize how big a story this would
become. (Years later, I heard the possibly apocryphal
tale of how a young reporter took out his guitar in the
newsroom and started playing "Imagine," only to be

shouted down by some of the older, grumpy editors.)

In the days after, I bought every newspaper I could find, stayed glued to TV reports by day and radio by night. The one thing that stuck with me through the confusion, anger and sadness was that I was not alone. People my age, older and some younger, felt the same sense of loss, across the globe.

Yoko called for a worldwide 10 minutes of silence on Sunday, Dec. 14, at 2 p.m., New York time. There would be gatherings around the world, including Central Park, across the street from the Dakota.

I wasn't going to miss it. My parents, surprisingly, gave me no argument. I could go, as long as I stuck with my friends and looked after my brother. They gave us carfare, $5 mugger money and another $5 to keep tucked in a sneaker in case of an emergency.

So we got off the subway, walked past the Dakota, a foreboding Gothic-style building with gargoyles and an Edward Gorey-like eeriness. My first in-person glimpse of the Dakota awed me and gave me the creeps. A sea of bodies jammed the sidewalk on either side of W. 72nd Street, leaving us to push our way across the street and into the park, where the "official" vigil would take place at the Naumburg Bandshell.

Our crew included Big John (who was quite tall for his age – or any age), Little John (who was somewhat short) and Big Dave (who was not big – it was one of those ironic nicknames, like calling your obese pal "Tiny." But with a few years and a lot of weight lifting, Big Dave would grow into his moniker).

Though thousands had started gathering the

day before, we managed to nudge our way well into the crowd, getting within about 50 yards of the Bandshell. Not that there was much to see: a simple black-and-white picture on an easel of John, arms crossed, in his sleeveless "New York City" T-shirt, staring back defiantly at a crowd awash in gloom. Many, including Big Dave, lugged radios, spurring impromptu sing-alongs that somehow melded into one another, even if the songs weren't always the same.

The smell of pot, which, for our crew, usually heralded that the neighborhood bad guys were lurking ahead, wafted non-threateningly through the brisk air, mingling with the scent of impending snowfall. The adults around us, stoned and otherwise, looked out for us, sharing food and drink. Little John, using size to his advantage, got a better view atop the shoulders of one aging hippie.

My strongest memory, frankly, is needing to pee, but literally having no place to go. Finally, around 1:30 p.m., John's music began playing over a loud-speaker. I'm pretty sure "In My Life," was the last song, ending at 2 p.m., and followed by silence, save for the fluttering blades of TV station helicopters overhead. I sat, closed my eyes and bowed my head. As a Catholic school veteran, I was used to being still and quiet, and having to keep my mind occupied while I was supposed to be praying.

For the first time, at least in a small way, I started to think about the future. I wanted a girlfriend. I wanted to play guitar well, and learn every Beatle song. I wanted the hostages to come home from Iran.

I wanted recently elected Ronald Reagan to disappear after his first term as president. I wanted nuclear weapons to disappear along with him. I wanted to be able to walk in my neighborhood without worrying about getting jumped. I really wanted that girlfriend, and I wanted her to love the Beatles as much as I did. But most of all, I wanted to open my eyes and find that the last six days had been a bad dream.

The flap-flap-flap of the choppers gave way to the opening chords of "Imagine." The crowd rose together, and strangers held hands, becoming a swaying human chain, broken only by those whose arms cradled the weeping.

After the song, the crowd began to disperse, with many turning west, probably planning to walk past the Dakota. We chose the path of least resistance, heading east, hoping to find somewhere to pee. We trod in silence, climbing to the top of a hill behind the Bandshell that gave us a view of the throng we had escaped. Big Dave turned on his radio. Just as John and Yoko's "Happy Xmas" began playing, snow started falling. "It's a sign!" Big Dave said excitedly.

Then we saw another kind of sign below us. A stoned guy in an Army jacket staggered into a group of cops, and shoved one. Suddenly, three cops started beating the man with nightsticks, in a 30-second or so flurry, until he was face down and handcuffed behind his back. "That ain't right!" yelled Big Dave, a little over a decade from becoming a cop – the kind who knows the value of restraint.

A denim-clad man in his 30s, standing behind

us, sighed and said, "I guess the Sixties are over."

The next year on Dec. 8, I returned to Central Park, this time alone and not knowing what to expect. The spot just inside the park that later would be re-christened Strawberry Fields was filled with fans, playing guitars, holding candles and flowers they had hoped to leave in front of the Dakota.

I would repeat the ritual over the years, alone and with various friends and loved ones, looking for some answers or solace, but usually coming away feeling cold and empty. Yoko sometimes would send down coffee, wave from her window or send a message to the crowd. But eventually, she began spending the day elsewhere.

Strawberry Fields didn't have many happy associations for me. There was a certain comfort when Theresa and I took Ella there after George died, but that was a different Beatle, a very different time, a very different kind of death.

I began to wonder whether I was making a mistake as Ella and I walked into the park 25 years to the day after John's murder. The turnout was the biggest I'd seen since the first anniversary vigil. Thanks to both the crowd and the cops, the line leading up the "Imagine" mosaic was as orderly as it was long. As we got closer, the candles made it almost seem like we were approaching a round patch of daylight, to a soundtrack of Beatles songs provided by hundreds of voices and dozens of jangling acoustic guitars.

"I can't see!" Ella said.

Someone overheard her. "Hey, there's a little girl trying to get in!" a woman said, and the message began to travel up the line.

Suddenly, cops cleared us a path. We stopped a moment and took in the light, flowers, photos and fan art that obscured the mosaic.

I looked into those gray-blue eyes. She was smiling. Ella was cold and tired – but happy. For her, it was another fun Beatle day: full of music, nice people, a certain amount of physical discomfort and a pleasant surprise. For her, this gathering represented a celebration.

In that moment, 25 years of sorrow lifted. Believing in yesterday is fine, but living for the moment and embracing the future is where it's at.

I was thinking about the future that night when I extracted from Ella a vow I hope she'll keep.

"I need you to make me a promise," I told her. "I took you here tonight. I want you to take me here in 25 years, on Dec. 8, 2030.

"When I'm 64."

Epilogue: Life Goes On

Ella's mood was as grey as the Hamburg sky outside the modest Turkish restaurant where the three of us sat in silence on a late afternoon in April 2012, nibbling on unusually crunchy and tasty falafel, watching a soccer game on a huge TV screen. We were killing time while the rain fell. We'd arrived in the seaport city a couple hours earlier after taking the high-speed ICE train from Berlin, exhausted but exhilarated from a four-day tour of the German capital. We were finishing up our vacation with a 36-hour stay in Hamburg, which rivals perhaps only Liverpool in its place in Beatledom.

The young, unknown Beatles had played all-night gigs in Hamburg's sleazy red-light district, earning their stripes as musicians and gaining a certain toughness that would help gird them for the mayhem to come. As John once said, "I might have been born in Liverpool – but I grew up in Hamburg."

Ella, at 15, was just two years younger than George when he, John, Paul, Pete Best and Stuart Sutcliffe arrived for their first stint in Hamburg in 1960. She wasn't exactly a tough kid, but she'd done some growing up – especially musically. With the Brooklyn Youth Chorus, she performed on stages of Radio City Musical Hall, Lincoln Center and, after a lot of practice, practice, practice, Carnegie Hall. She left the chorus, against our wishes, not in an act of rebellion, but because she felt she was stretching herself too thin.

Her heart remained dedicated to rock and roll: At 12, she sang "Me and Bobby McGee" on CBS' "The Early Show," backed by her School of Rock pals. She plays gigs – rock, jazz, classical – with various bands all over town as her musical tastes have expanded to Led Zeppelin, Gentle Giant, Frank Zappa, Bach and jazz vocal and bass powerhouse Esperanza Spalding.

Top New York club-scene musicians led by Jesse Krakow recruited Ella to play bass and sing in Captain Beefheart and Spinal Tap tributes, sharing the bill, with among others, the great Nona Hendrix. One of her bands, Doomsday Diaries, opened variously for Zebra ("Tell Me What You Want") and Ellen Foley (of "Paradise by the Dashboard Light" fame). She's even performed avant-garde compositions at a theater in Soho (Yoko would be proud).

Ella's always welcome to sit in with The Meetles, a delightfully quirky Beatles cover band that performs regularly in Grand Central Terminal and Penn Station. We met The Meetles through our Beatles Meetup group, which formed after 9/11, and comes together at Beatle-related concerts, fan conventions and other gatherings. Ella, from about age 8, became the musical mascot of the Meet-up group, playing bass at annual sing-alongs.

But at a get-together shortly before our trip to Germany, Ella declined exhortations to join in and wound up sitting in the back alone, refusing to talk to anyone, looking miserable and sullen. That's the same way she looked a couple weeks earlier when I asked her why she chose to play in a School of Rock White Stripes tribute show over a Beatles show ("That's for little kids," she snarled). The same way she looked when I told her I was writing this book ("If you have to do this, can't you just change our names? Or at least mine?"). The same way she looked as we sat in the falafel joint in Hamburg, as Theresa and I couldn't wait for the rain to stop so we could begin our latest plunge into latent Beatlemania.

In between falafel bites, I broke the silence by asking for ideas for next year's trip. That was something of a tradition: We always brainstormed our next vacation while on vacation. We'd first talked about a possible Germany jaunt a year before on our previous spring break journey to Nashville, New Orleans and Memphis, where Ella drew cheers on Beale Street while jamming with veteran blues musicians.

Ella's face turned from moody teenager scowl to a very adult-looking grim bearer of bad news. "I want to go to Italy next year," she said.

"That's great," Theresa replied. "I think we should..."

"Not with you," Ella interrupted. "With kids from school. The Italian department does a trip there every year."

We were taken aback – proud, saddened, a little relieved that she's finally striking out on her own a bit, and somewhat annoyed (does she think we're made of money?). At least it was an honest moment. Also a bittersweet one: A phase of our lives was ending, a short walk from where life began to take off for the young

Beatles.

As the rain let up, we trod through Hamburg's notorious Reeperbahn, a neighborhood in transition with sleazy bars and sex shops smack up against a growing hipster scene, which, if I understood the German sign correctly, included an aromatherapy spa. We walked to Grosse Freiheit, the nastiest street in the city (save for the closed-off block nearby where prostitutes advertise their wares in store windows, a la Amsterdam).

The Beatles were once staples on Grosse Freiheit, playing the Kaiserkeller and the Star-Club, where they became the joint's first act 50 years earlier on this very day. The Star-Club was long gone, but the Kaiserkeller still rocked. We'd scored tickets to an anniversary concert starring what's left of Liverpool groups like The Searchers, The Undertakers and The Quarrymen. Even Pete Best was in town with his new band.

Ella walked ahead of us as we passed seedy establishments with names like Dollhouse and Safari, her hunched shoulders and quickening pace betraying her discomfort. We got to end of the block where the Kaiserkeller sits. But our eyes were drawn to the establishment next door with a kitty-cat-themed neon sign that blared: "Funky Pussy Club."

Theresa and I struggled to stifle giggles. Ella, in front of us, turned away and we saw her back convulse. Was she crying? She looked across the street to see the only non-club on the block – an 18th-century church, the same one where the Beatles (or at least

John, depending on who's doing the telling) supposedly would greet congregants on Sunday mornings by peeing out the Kaiserkeller's windows after playing all night Saturday. Ella stood in the middle of the street turning from one to another, and finally swung around toward us and began laughing until the tears flowed. We joined her.

The happiest moments of our lives together come from music and laughter, often found in unexpected places. The Beatles have given us plenty of both, prompting us to embark on adventures that have drawn us closer. John, Paul, George and Ringo also have given us the confidence and inspiration to explore our own modest dreams. So yes, the manic travel and going to every convention and Beatles-related concert is bound to abate. In some ways, we're three different people now. Better people, we hope.

Theresa has added theatrical producer to her resume, staging an immigration-themed musical called "Liberty." A couple weeks after our Hamburg trip, her 50th birthday coincided with the news that "The Gershwins' Porgy and Bess," her first Broadway show as an associate producer, had been nominated for 10 Tony Awards. It would go on to collect two statues, including one for Best Musical Revival.

My life is changing in more humble ways: I'm writing songs again and playing with a band called The Monotone Assassins. The four of us have kids who are great musicians and love much of the same music we do. We're not a Beatles cover group, but two of our big numbers are "I'm Down" and "One After 909." I even sing a little, though, vocally I'm the Ringo of the band. The closest I get to a showstopper is my version of Ringo's version of Carl Perkins' "Honey Don't."

Ella's a relatively typical teenager. She bickers with her mother frequently, and only agrees with her in pointing out when I'm wrong. She's growing more confident and independent, going to concerts featuring bands we've never heard of with bandmates and classmates from New York's LaGuardia High School, the so-called "Fame" school, where she plays double bass in an orchestra and a jazz ensemble. She's already researching colleges, with an eye on a possible music-related career. Life is changing, quickly.

We choose our Beatle moments more selectively now. One must is the Fab Faux's annual post-Christmas residency at a fine New York club called City Winery, a jaunt I hope we'll make for years to come. The third of October will always be a day we treasure, even if there isn't a cake – like the one rolled out for Ringo during his 70th birthday concert at Radio City Music Hall when Paul surprised everybody by bounding on the stage and playing "Birthday," with his old bandmate on drums.

We'd been to Radio City a few weeks before to see the kids from "Glee," which, by that time, Ella had outgrown and Theresa hadn't. From start to finish, headache-inducing screams filled the theater, making us feel like we were in a subway tunnel with the train bearing down. "This is what it must have been like to be at a Beatles concert," Theresa said afterward, our ears still ringing as we waited for the F train home.

When Paul strode out onto the stage at Ringo's show, concertgoers from six to well past 70 erupted so furiously that the hall shook, making the "Glee" mania sound like a pin drop. We turned to one another and smiled. "*This* is what it must have been like with the Beatles," Ella said later.

Probably not, but this would be as close as we'd get. At least we got there together.

These days, we most often intersect in our happily busy lives on Sunday mornings, when we wake up to "Breakfast With the Beatles," hosted on New York radio station 104.3 FM by Ken Dashow, a Brooklyn native and Beatle fanatic whose show is an intergenerational celebration of the greatest music ever made.

Ken's "Breakfast" is filled with call-ins and emails from fans giving shout outs to friends and loved ones. We've sent requests over the years. Ken played "English Tea" for Ella to mark the first anniversary of her meeting Paul. For us, the radio program is as close as we come to a weekly reflection and spiritual experience (sorry, Sister Beata).

Even as we take up different places in the house, the music we love pours out of us. One Sunday morning not too long ago, we milled about the kitchen in our separate little worlds – Theresa tapping on her computer keyboard, Ella studying at the breakfast table, me standing at the kitchen counter, flipping through the papers. Without looking up, we fell into a reasonably tight three-part harmony on the song that bests sums up the push and pull of changing lives – growing up while hopefully never growing old, growing apart but always tied by a bond strengthened by the music we share. The words flowed from our lips as one: "*Hello, hello. I don't know why you say goodbye, I say hello.*"

Acknowledgements: With a Lot of Help From My Friends (And Family)

One thing you quickly learn when you embark on a book about John, Paul, George and Ringo is that everybody has a Beatles story. Many stem from childhood family sing-alongs, first albums or movies. Others would have fit nicely in David Letterman's old "Brush With Fame" segment.

Joanna Hernandez met John and Yoko in 1978 when she was a young mom working the ticket booth at Manhattan's Ziegfeld Theater. Instead of going right in to see "The Boys From Brazil," John spent a few minutes asking Joanna about her life, even as she could barely contain her excitement.

Nanci Davis got a friendly hug from Yoko a couple years ago in front of the Dakota.

Tim Harper, who is more responsible than anyone for bringing this book to life, is more responsible than anyone for spreading the "Paul is dead" rumor. It was Tim's article, written in 1969 for the Drake Times-Delphic student paper while an undergrad at Drake University in Des Moines, Iowa, that got countless millions, stoned and otherwise, scouring album covers for clues and playing records backwards.

Tim started the CUNY Journalism Press at the City University of New York Graduate School of Journalism, where I am blessed to work. This book took shape in wonderful long-form narrative classes Tim organized for faculty, staff and alumni.

Among the talented folks who generously shared their insight during those invaluable sessions: Heather Appel, Jenni Avins, Linnea Covington, Prue Clarke, Lois DeSocio, Barbara Gray, Joanna Hernandez, Carol Kelly, Daryl Khan, Valerie Lapinski, Sherry Mazzocchi, Melinda Wenner Moyer, Carla Murphy, Chris Prentice, Diana Robertson, Indrani Sen, Maureen Sullivan, Wayne Svoboda and Robert Voris. Diana was kind enough to be my first beta reader. Indrani and Daryl offered tips that helped me get through my early struggles with chapter structure.

Thanks to Wendell Jamieson and Helene Stapinski who gave me great advice early on – it took me a while to listen, but I hope this book proves them right. Glenn Lewis also offered much-appreciated initial encouragement during summer lunches as I recovered from a back injury in 2008. The irrepressible Mr. Lewis helped get my mind off my discomfort and onto this project. So did David Chiu, a former student who wisely taught his former teacher. Mitch Trinka, a student-turned-colleague, proved again that his talent is exceeded only by his generosity.

My Monotone Assassins bandmates Tom Jenkins, Gary Richman and Greg B. Smith reinforced my belief that growing up doesn't mean you have to grow old – and music is proof.

My cousin, the artist Raffael Cavallaro, is responsible for the brilliant cover illustration that graces this book. Gabe Stuart of Bayberry Books exhibited great skill and patience in helping an amateur become a first-time publisher. John Oakes' belief in this project came along just as I was starting to lose faith. His incredible publishing seminar at CUNY gave me some of the tools I needed to get this book off my hard drive and into your hands. Rosaleen Ortiz helped bring the vision for the book onto the Web.

Thanks to my colleagues at NBC – especially Greg Gittrich and Dick Belsky, who gave me an outlet to write about my pop culture obsessions, and teased me about my Beatlemania even as they always posted my pieces. I'm grateful to all my colleagues from my 15 years at the New York Daily News, my hometown paper, where the byline I was most thrilled to see was Ella's the morning after she met Paul.

I've been incredibly fortunate to work with some of the best editors and reporters in journalism – far too many to name without filling another book. But special thanks are due to Steve Shepard and Judy Watson, the best bosses I've ever had, and to the rest of my always generous colleagues at the CUNY J-School.

I'd also like to thank the many agents who took the time to read my query, proposal and, in some cases, manuscript. Some of you were encouraging, even in rejection.

Susan Ainsleigh's report from our 2005 Magical History Tour to London and Liverpool, led by the unfailingly enthusiastic Charles Rosensay!!!, helped spur some great memories. Thanks to Xiomara Martinez-White for her fine proofreading (and soccer-related insight). She scoured the book line-by-line as did my colleague Barbara Gray, and Theresa and Ella who didn't hesitate to tell me when I got something wrong. Any errors within are my responsibility alone.

Forgive me any unintended omissions – if you're mentioned in the book, consider yourself thanked. Even if I missed a few of you, you know who you are. This book is meant as a thank-you note not only to John, Paul, George and Ringo, but to fellow fans and the many of you to whom I am forever in debt, in ways large and small.

The great thing about Beatle stories is that new ones pop up all the time. During one of the early sessions in Tim Harper's long-form narrative class, Carla Murphy, a smart young journalist born in Barbados, admitted to knowing little about the Beatles. I sent her "Revolver," via iTunes, as a thank-you for bringing a fresh eye to my chapters-in-progress, which took for granted that everybody breathes the Beatles. "This is awesome!" she wrote.

"Awesome" doesn't begin to describe Theresa and Ella, to whom I'm forever grateful for all the unforgettable stories they've given me to tell – and for all the future memories on the road that stretches out ahead.

Jere Hester
Brooklyn, N.Y.
August 2013

About the Author

Jere Hester is founding director of the award-winning NYCity News Service at the City University of New York Graduate School of Journalism. Hester, a former city editor at the New York Daily News, also writes a pop culture column for NBC Local Integrated Media. He is a lifelong resident of Brooklyn, N.Y., where he lives with his wife, Theresa Wozunk, and their daughter, Ella, in a house filled with music.

Made in the USA
San Bernardino, CA
09 March 2016